NEVER GET ANGRY AGAIN

ALSO BY DAVID J. LIEBERMAN

Never Be Lied to Again

Instant Analysis

Get Anyone to Do Anything

Make Peace with Anyone

How to Change Anybody

NEVER GET ANGRY AGAIN

DAVID J. LIEBERMAN, PH.D.

The Foolproof Way to Stay Calm and in Control
in Any Conversation or Situation

ST. MARTIN'S PRESS
NEW YORK

NEVER GET ANGRY AGAIN. Copyright © 2017 by David J. Lieberman. All rights reserved. Printed in the United States of America. For information, address St. Martin's Press, 175 Fifth Avenue, New York, N.Y. 10010.

www.stmartins.com

The Library of Congress Cataloging-in-Publication Data is available upon request.

ISBN 978-1-250-15439-2 (hardcover)
ISBN 978-1-250-15440-8 (ebook)

Our books may be purchased in bulk for promotional, educational, or business use. Please contact your local bookseller or the Macmillan Corporate and Premium Sales Department at 1-800-221-7945, extension 5442, or by email at MacmillanSpecialMarkets@macmillan.com.

First Edition: January 2018

10 9 8 7 6 5 4 3 2 1

CONTENTS

INTRODUCTION 1

PART I

THE REAL REASON YOU ARE SO ANGRY 7

    1. How Perspective Takes Shape 9

    2. Angry with Ourselves, Angry at the World 13

    3. Isolated from Ourselves, Disconnected from Others 19

    4. Step Right Up and Choose Your Reality 25

PART II

THE COST OF LIVING, THE PRICE OF ESCAPING 35

    5. Why Smart People Do Dumb Things 37

    6. A Fight to the Death 43

    7. Reality Isn't Going Anywhere 47

    8. The Meaning of Pleasure, the Pleasure of Meaning 55

CONTENTS

PART III

MAKING SENSE OF PAIN AND SUFFERING 61

    9. Here Comes the Pain 63

    10. Why Good Things Happen to Bad People 67

    11. Staying Sane in an Insane World 71

PART IV

MAKE PEACE WITH THE PAST, FOR GOOD 79

    12. Planes of Acceptance 81

    13. Trauma, Tragedy, and Triggers 85

    14. It's Not Too Late to Have a Happy Childhood 89

    15. My Apologies, Please 99

PART V

HOW TO LOVE BEING ALIVE 107

    16. A Date with Destiny 109

    17. Becoming Extraordinary 113

    18. Escaping the Trap of Procrastination 119

PART VI

**RECLAIMING OURSELVES AND REDEFINING
OUR BOUNDARIES** 123

    19. Redrawing the Lines with Boundary Breachers 125

    20. How to Talk to People Who Don't Listen 131

    21. Speak Now, or Forever Be in Pieces 137

    22. Successful Relationships with Impossible People 145

CONTENTS

PART VII

ADVANCED PSYCHOLOGICAL STRATEGIES

TO LIVE ANGER FREE 151

   23. The Power of Neuroplasticity 153

   24. Change Your Self-Concept, Change Your Life 159

   25. Taking Advantage of the Mind/Body Connection 165

   26. Getting Real with Meditation and Visualization 173

   27. In the Heat of the Moment 179

   28. The Magnitude of Gratitude 187

   29. The Anger Games 195

   30. Game Day 201

SPECIAL NOTE TO READERS 207

ACKNOWLEDGMENTS 209

ENDNOTES. 211

ABOUT THE AUTHOR 225

NEVER GET ANGRY AGAIN

INTRODUCTION

Let's face it, if anger-management techniques were effective, you wouldn't be reading this book. You've probably tried it all: positive self-talk, punching a pillow, and reminding yourself that no good will come from getting angry. But the next time you feel your blood boiling or you start to fly into a blind range, see how well counting to ten works for you.

These clumsy attempts to maintain calmness are often futile and sometimes emotionally draining. Anger-management books typically feature these tried-and-not-true methods, along with generic case studies, personal anecdotes, and bumper-sticker slogans. The fact is, either something bothers us (causing anxiety, frustration, or anger) or it doesn't. Yes, our objective is to remain calm, but we can better accomplish this by not becoming agitated in the first place. When we fight the urge to blow up or melt down, we struggle against our own nature.

THE MILLION-DOLLAR QUESTION
What makes some people able to handle life's ups and downs, the twists and turns, bumps and bruises with steadfast calm and composure, while others become incensed at the slightest insult, fall

apart when facing a minor frustration, and blow out of proportion a mild disappointment?

In a word: perspective.

Imagine a small child playing with a toy that suddenly breaks. The child's whole world shatters, and she may respond by crying or becoming despondent, sad, or even angry. The child fails to appreciate, let alone recognize, all of the goodness in her life: that she is still being clothed, fed, loved, and taken care of—not to mention that an entire world exists outside of her own smaller world. The child's parents know the broken toy has no real relevance because they have perspective that the child lacks.

Intellectually, we may recognize the unimportance and insignificance of whatever made us angry. Yet the qualities that most of us strive to exemplify—such as objectivity and patience—are lost to frustration when, in a hurry, we encounter a checkout clerk with a trainee name tag staring at the cash register as if it were the cockpit of the space shuttle. We try to maintain our cool, but negative emotions surface and, once sparked, blaze. Now we face an uphill battle.

Perspective lies at the crux of our response and explains why we often feel irritated in the heat of the moment. After a few minutes, our anger subsides. A few hours later, we feel less angry, and in a few days, we wonder why we got so bothered in the first place. Time provides perspective, allowing us to see the situation with clarity. Likewise, as we grow and mature, we look back on our lives and realize that the summer camp we thought we *must* attend, the person we thought we *must* be friends with, or the office job we thought we *must* be offered are no longer *musts*. Without perspective, we are forever like a child with a broken toy.

THE MILLION-DOLLAR ANSWER

Mark Twain wrote, "Comedy is tragedy plus time." When we discover how to shift our perspective, we see today's events through the wiser, more balanced lens of tomorrow. Once we can recognize—in the moment—what really matters, we no longer need to force ourselves to remain calm. Our thoughts, feelings, and responses to any situation reshape themselves. Negative emotions like impatience, insecurity, and anger dissolve—not because we fight to control our emotions but, rather, because we see the situation for what it really is.

Of course, the question we still face is, "How do we manage what is relevant?" Yes, we know we shouldn't "sweat the small stuff," and the only reason we do is that we lack perspective. But what about serious things, such as an illness, an injustice, or a trauma? Objectively, they *are* a big deal. To handle such crises with equanimity, we learn to pull back the lens even further, to find peace of mind regardless of the present or pending situation; and gain the presence of mind to take responsible action.

Metaphorically speaking, typical anger-management tools are akin to weed killer: You have to keep spraying all of the time, every time, to keep weeds from sprouting up—and no matter how vigilant you are, you'll still miss plenty, and you are left exhausted. *Never Get Angry Again* explains how to pull up weeds by their roots by looking at reality—ourselves, our lives, and our relationships—with optimum perspective and emotional clarity.

Through a comprehensive, holistic lens, we reveal and illuminate the causes and components of anger. These often include the gaping hole in our self-esteem due to a rotten (chaotic or traumatic) childhood, failing or failed relationships with those important to us, or living a life that lacks any real passion and joy—all fueled by an undercurrent of resentment as we wonder, where is God in all of this? *Life is unfair, so either He's not in charge, He doesn't care, or He simply hates me.* Not exactly self-esteem boosters or anger reducers.

Certainly, even with the proper perspective, we can get caught up in the moment. High-intensity situations can provoke us to throw reason and rationale right out the window, as our emotions erupt before we even know what's happening. Yet it doesn't have to be like this. Should an errant weed pop up under extreme circumstances, you can still maintain complete control. By using cutting-edge research from the field of neuroplasticity, you can literally rewire your brain to automatically take over, even when you feel as if you're losing your mind.

Now, as the saying goes, "it takes two to tango." While a challenging life circumstance is one thing, the truth is, we wouldn't have to manage our anger if the people in our lives would manage their stupidity. Some folks—family, friends, and coworkers—just push our buttons. In keeping with my penchant for the practical, you will learn step-by-step strategies to redraw boundaries, quash personality conflicts, and navigate difficult relationships to maintain (or reclaim) your sanity and eradicate a breeding ground for anger and frustration.

UNMASKING THE ENEMY

Various techniques will help us succeed in controlling our anger, but they can't create awareness. Only the complete recognition of the apparatus—and the foolishness and futility—of anger will organically motivate us to keep our calm. For this reason, the first several sections of this book are descriptive; they explain the psychological dynamics of anger and of human nature. The latter sections are prescriptive, offering a range of psychological tools and techniques to win the ground war. But do not underestimate the power of understanding the enemy, anger. In any anger-provoking situation, we would love to ask ourselves, *Why am I really getting angry?* But of course, we can't ask the question because we aren't thinking; we are only feeling. At that moment, nobody's home, and this is the fatal flaw in the tradition of anger management. However, when we wholly embrace the answer to this question with every fiber of our being *before* the situation arises, even when we lose perspective, the truth is baked into our very nature, and a calm and controlled response becomes second nature.

THE TAKEAWAY

Never Get Angry Again shows you how to permanently reorient your perspective. This will automatically take life's little things right off your radar, and the big stuff will never again manifest as fiery fits of uncontrollable anger or rage, but instead be instantly viewed through the lens of authentic acceptance. Discover the easy way to live anger-free and never get angry again—unless you want to.

PART I

THE REAL REASON YOU ARE SO ANGRY

1
How Perspective Takes Shape

Three forces within us are often at odds with one another: the soul, the ego, and the body. In short, the soul seeks to do what is right; the ego wants to be right and see itself in an optimal light; and the body just wants to escape from it all. When you make any decision in life:

- You can choose what feels good.
- You can choose what makes you look good.
- You can choose to do what is good or right.

Doing what feels comfortable or enjoyable is a body drive. Excesses of this type are overeating or oversleeping—in effect, doing something merely because it feels good. When we act based on an ego drive, it can run the gamut from telling a joke at someone else's expense to making a lavish purchase that's beyond our means. When the ego reigns, we are not drawn to what *is* good, but to what makes us *look* good.

We gain self-esteem only when we make responsible choices and do what is right—this is a soul-oriented (moral or conscience) choice. Indeed, this is how self-esteem and self-control are intertwined. Emotional freedom doesn't mean doing whatever we feel like doing; rather, it is doing what we truly want to do, despite our desires at the moment. Imagine being on a diet and suddenly feeling the urge to eat a piece of chocolate. We fight the temptation but eventually give in. Is this freedom or slavery? We felt like eating a piece of chocolate, and we did it. Did we like how we felt afterward? When we choose responsibly, we exercise self-control and increase our self-esteem.

DO GOOD TO FEEL GOOD

Each time we sacrifice what is responsible because we can't rise above the whims of an impulse or sell ourselves out to win the praise or approval of others, we lose self-respect. When we routinely succumb to immediate gratification or live to protect and project an image, we become angry with ourselves and ultimately feel empty inside. To quiet the unconscious gnawing that says, *I don't like me*, we do whatever we can to feel good. We long to love ourselves, but instead we lose ourselves. Unable to invest in our own well-being, we spiral downward to the hollow, self-destructive refuge of activities that take us away from the pain: excessive eating, alcohol or drug abuse, and meaningless diversions and excursions. These ethereal delights mask our self-contempt, and because the happiness we seek instead results in greater pain, we descend further into despair—and into hiding.

Let's look at this another way: Have you ever tried to have a pleasant conversation with someone you didn't like? Or to spend an hour or entire day with someone who gets on your nerves? It's almost painful. What if you lived with that person—and that person happened to be you? Everything in life is draining for the person who doesn't like who he has become. It's like working for a boss we despise; even the most minor task triggers annoyance.

Would we work hard for or invest in—let alone love and respect—an ungrateful, out-of-control person? You might try to quiet or distract him with pointless pursuits or endless entertainment, or even help him to get lost in a haze of abusive behaviors—as long as you don't have to face him, much less help him.

To the extent that we don't love ourselves, our willingness to endure short-term pain for long-term gain wanes. Who wants to put in effort, enduring heartache and hardship, for someone whom they don't even like? This mind-set is understandable but quite problematic. When we too often shirk our obligations and shun new opportunities, we lose more than we might imagine. Studies show that our tendency to avoid the pain inherent in taking responsibility for our lives is at the core of anger, and is central to nearly every emotional ailment, including anxiety, depression, and addiction.[1]

PERSPECTIVE = MENTAL HEALTH

As our behavior becomes increasingly reckless and irresponsible, the ego swells to compensate for feelings of guilt, insecurity, and shame. Our perspective narrows, and we see more of the self and less of the world—which makes us ever more sensitive and unstable. To the degree that we refuse to accept the truth about ourselves and our lives—and overcome our laziness and fear of pain—the ego engages to "protect" us, and it shifts the blame elsewhere. In other words, *If there is nothing wrong with me, then there must be something wrong with you;* or *the world is unfair;* or *people are out to get me.* Seedlings of neuroses and paranoia then take root. For us to remain unblemished in our own minds, we are forced to distort the world around us, and if our grasp on reality is flawed, then our adjustment to life will suffer.[2]

When a person loses his sanity—the ability to see, accept, and respond to his world—it means he has lost all perspective. Emotional instability—the seat of anger—is fundamentally a lack of clarity, the degree to which the ego infects us.

> Responsible (soul-oriented) choice → self-esteem increases → ego shrinks → perspective widens → undistorted reality → see and accept the truth (even when difficult or painful) = positive emotional health → act responsibly

> Irresponsible (ego-oriented/overindulgent body) choice → self-esteem decreases → ego expands → perspective narrows→ distorted reality → unable/ unwilling to see and accept truth (when difficult or painful) = negative mental health→ act irresponsibly

2
Angry with Ourselves, Angry at the World

None of us wants to admit, even to ourselves, that we are selfish or lazy, much less a failure or flawed. The ego is thus equipped with an elaborate array of shields and buffers—defense mechanisms— to thwart the harshness of reality. Of course, instead of protecting us (rather than itself), these defense mechanisms lead to increased instability and insecurity. And the wider the chasm between the truth and our ability to accept it, the more fragile our emotional health becomes. In *Reality Therapy,* Dr. William Glasser writes:

> In their unsuccessful effort to fulfill their needs, no matter what behavior they choose, all patients have a common characteristic: they all deny the reality of the world around them. . . . Whether it is a partial denial or the total blotting out of all of reality of the chronic backward patient in the state hospital, the denial of some or all of reality is common to patients. Therapy will be successful when they are able to give up denying the world and recognize that reality exists but that they must fulfill their needs within its framework.[1]

Our ego colors the world so that we remain untarnished. Before we airbrush reality, however, a collision occurs in the unaccessed caverns of our unconscious, between truth and falsehood, producing the psychological phenomenon *cognitive dissonance*: the feeling of uncomfortable tension and stress that comes from holding two contradictory ideas simultaneously. It is the by-product of tension between the soul and ego—when we choose to either accept reality or reduce dissonance by any number of defense mechanisms. The most common of these are avoidance, denial, or justification.

Shopaholics are often a good example of cognitive dissonance. Though cognizant of the dangers associated with this addiction, shopaholics may reduce the tension by: (a) avoiding the issue, i.e., putting all expenses on a credit card and not focusing on the money spent; (b) denying that they are addicted and cannot stop—that it is as if their vehicle drives into the nearest mall of its own volition; (c) rationalizing their shopping habits ("If I don't spend time out of the house, I will go off my diet"); or, the heathiest and most difficult (d) accepting the truth and taking steps to get the needed help.

> "Drew Westen and his colleagues (2006) found that the 'reasoning areas of the brain virtually shut down when a person is confronted with dissonant information and the emotion circuits of the brain light up happily when consonance is restored.'[2] As Westen put it, people twirl the 'cognitive kaleidoscope' until the pieces fall into the pattern they want to see, and then the brain repays them by activating circuits involved in pleasure. It seems that the feeling of cognitive dissonance can literally make your brain hurt!"[3]

That's why the ego seizes any opportunity to reconcile internal conflict. The following anecdote illustrates this process, particularly when our self-concept is on the line.

A man woke up one day convinced that he was a zombie. When he told his wife he was a zombie, she tried to talk him out of this outrageous opinion.

"You are not a zombie!" she said.

"I am a zombie," he answered.

"What makes you think you're a zombie?" she asked rhetorically.

"Don't you think zombies know they are zombies?" he answered with great sincerity.

His wife realized she wasn't getting anywhere, so she called his mother and told her what was going on. His mother tried to help.

"I'm your mother. Wouldn't I know if I gave birth to a zombie?"

"You didn't," he explained. "I became a zombie later."

"I didn't raise my son to be a zombie or especially to think he is a zombie," his mother pleaded.

"Nonetheless, I am a zombie," he said, unmoved by his mother's appeal to his identity and sense of guilt.

Later that day, his wife called a psychiatrist.

The receptionist gave the wife an emergency appointment, and within the hour, the husband was in the psychiatrist's office.

"So, you think you are a zombie?" the psychiatrist asked.

"I know I am a zombie," the man said.

"Tell me, do zombies bleed?" the psychiatrist asked.

"Of course not," said the man. "Zombies are the living dead. They don't bleed." The man felt a little annoyed at the psychiatrist's patronizing question.

"Well, watch this," said the psychiatrist, picking up a pin. He took the man's finger and made a tiny pinprick. The man looked at his finger with great amazement and said nothing for three or four minutes.

"What do you know?" the man finally said. "Zombies *do* bleed!"[4]

THE MASK THAT DOESN'T COME OFF

Denying reality comes with a price. Exhausted and on edge, our ego edits our world to eliminate anything that will hurt or reveal us, either to ourselves or to others. Preoccupied with potential threats to our self-image, we are on constant guard. We hide behind a carefully crafted façade, and the identity that we build to shield ourselves soon becomes a shell encasing us. Over time, we fall into a hellish gap of unrealized potential, our true self weakens, and we feel hollow inside. We no longer live for ourselves. We exist only to protect our image, the ego. This includes all of the games we play and the masks we wear to show the rest of the world what we believe is the necessary persona.

We may not even realize how much of our attitude and behavior—indeed, our values and beliefs—we style to avoid self-reflection, to compensate for self-hatred, and to project an image that betrays neither. In the exchange, we lose ourselves, contorting to the rules demanded by others to win their praise. Unsurprisingly, we never feel truly satiated. When we don't love ourselves, we can't give love, and we can't feel loved. Even when the supply of affection and adulation is plentiful, we experience a different reality—an endless flow of tainted love. Ultimately, we remain empty and angry inside.

Imagine pouring water into a cup that has no bottom. As you pour in the water, the cup feels and looks full. As long as the cup is constantly being filled, we feel content. But the minute someone stops filling it (with undivided attention, respect, or adoration), the cup quickly empties, and we are left as thirsty as ever. A shattered cup will never be full, and our thirst can never be quenched, no matter how much we receive. King Solomon, the wisest of men, wrote, "A lacking on the inside can never be satisfied with something from the outside."[5] People who seek self-esteem from external sources can never be truly content. They are the very epitome of a bottomless pit.

We are hardwired to love ourselves, but when we can't nourish ourselves through good choices and thus gain self-respect, we turn to the rest of the world to feed us. We make a desperate but futile attempt to convert their love and respect into feelings of self-worth. Our ever-shifting self-image becomes a direct reflection of the world around us. Our mood is raw and vulnerable to every fleeting glance and passing comment.

We erroneously and frantically believe, *If they care about me, then maybe I'm worth something, and then maybe I can love me.* Yet it doesn't work, and herein lies the basis for many failed relationships. When we lack self-esteem, we push away the very people we so desperately want in our lives because we can't fathom why anyone would love someone as unlovable as ourselves. And whatever affection or kindness forces its way through to us, we hardly embrace it. Such overtures don't serve to comfort but, rather, to confuse us; and the ego's mandate is clear: reject others before they have a chance to reject us.

To compound matters, the less self-control we have, the more desperately we manipulate events and people around us, especially those closest to us—either overtly or passive-aggressively. We intuit that self-control fosters self-respect, so when we cannot control ourselves, we need to feel as if we are in control of someone, something, anything, to feel a sense of power (the intricacies of which are further detailed in Chapter 4). Low self-esteem can thus trigger a powerful unconscious desire to usurp authority, to overstep bounds, and to mistreat those who care about us. When we don't like who we are, we cannot help but become angry with ourselves. Then we take it out on the world around us and on the people who care most about us.

3

Isolated from Ourselves, Disconnected from Others

For better or worse, our emotional, spiritual, and physical well-being feasts on, and fuels, the quality of our relationships—past and present. The previous chapter explained that people with low self-esteem have difficulty receiving love; indeed, they cannot easily give love, either. We can only give what we have. We give love. We give respect. If we don't have it, what do we have to give?

GIVE AND TAKE

Love is limitless. A parent does not love her second child less because she already has one child. She loves each child, gives to each child, and does not run out of love. Compare this to someone who acquires a work of art that he "loves." Over time, his fascination with the piece wanes, and when he acquires a new work, all of his attention, affection, and joy are redirected from the old art to the new art because, in truth, he does not care for his art. He cares for himself, and his art makes him happy. He is not giving to his art; his art gives to him, and so he takes. A person may say, *"I love cookies."* He doesn't. He enjoys eating cookies. If he truly loved cookies, then he would keep them out of sight and safe. Love is not selfish.

Moving to a more profound scenario, it should come as no

surprise that anger is easily triggered when we focus on our own pain and how difficult life is for us. For instance, when faced with a present or impending loss, the egocentric person grieves less for the other, and more for himself. His loss. His guilt. His woe. The less the ego is involved, the less stuck we will become, because normal feelings of sadness are processed healthily rather than suppressed, masked, or channeled away from the healing process. Let's consider the four stages of grief: denial, anger, depression, and acceptance. The first three stages are ego-based. Only when we loosen the ego's grip can we move toward acceptance.

Herein lies the often-blurred distinction between lust and love. Lust is the opposite of love. When we lust after someone or something, our interest is purely selfish. We want to take, to feel complete. When we love, however, we focus on how we can give, and we do so happily and eagerly. When someone we love is in pain, we feel pain. When someone we lust after is in pain, however, our thoughts go to how it will affect us in terms of our own inconvenience or discomfort. *What does this mean for me, not you?*

When a person suffers from low self-esteem, he takes what he needs in an attempt to make himself feel whole, which is why the last person you want trying to love you is someone who doesn't love himself. This person cannot really love, he can only control and take. The more self-esteem we have, the more complete we are. Receiving, after all, is a natural and reciprocal consequence of giving. When we only take, however, to fill a constant void, we are left empty, and are forced to continue taking in a futile quest to feel fulfilled, which only reinforces our dependency and exhausts us emotionally and physically.

Since self-esteem endows us with the ability to both give and to receive, some people with low self-esteem may have great difficulty accepting favors and expressing gratitude because needing or receiving help can trigger feelings of inadequacy. If the discomfort is severe, he may develop hostile feelings toward the very person extending the offering, because the giver brings increased awareness to his insecurities and shortcomings.[1]

Through this paradigm, we learn how to tell whether someone has high or low self-esteem; it is reflected in how he treats himself *and* others. A person who lacks self-esteem may indulge in things to satisfy only his own desires, and he will not treat others particularly well (a product of an arrogant mentality). Alternatively, this person may cater to others because he craves their approval and respect, but he does not take care of his own needs (a product of the doormat mentality). Only someone who has higher self-esteem can give responsibly—love and respect—to both himself and others.

EMPATHY VS. SYMPATHY

This brings us to another marked distinction, between sympathy and empathy. The former means that we feel pity for a person's situation, but we are disinclined to exert ourselves to alleviate his plight. A person may be very sensitive to the suffering of others, but if he merely *sympathizes*, he is consumed with his own pain and is then motivated primarily to reduce *his own suffering*—usually by means of escapism and indulgence—rather than help the person who actually feels pain. He often wishes he were unaware of the sorrow around him so as not to suffer as a result.

The typical characteristics of the egocentric mentality are arrogance and bravado, but even a highly sensitive person who is seemingly void of ego can also be self-centered and selfish. He is absorbed in his own pain, filled with self-pity, and he can't feel anyone else's pain while drowning in his own. Such a person experiences no real connection to anyone outside of himself, despite his seemingly noble nature. Without genuine humility, he will not—cannot—burden himself unless he receives a larger payout in the form of acceptance or approval. His taking is disguised as giving. His fear is dressed up as love. (He may also be motivated by the need to assuage feelings of guilt or inadequacy, yet still, his aim is to reduce his own suffering, not someone else's).

Empathy, by comparison, is the capacity to share another's emotions and feel his pain, rather than to merely feel sorry for him. The person with empathy feels grateful for knowing about others' troubles because he genuinely wants to alleviate their suffering. Moral development, rather than just moral thinking, is what moves a person to altruistic behavior. In fact, sociopaths have been shown to possess excellent moral reasoning but feel no need to act befittingly—this requires empathy.[2]

Parenthetically, the ease with which we rise above our own problems and shift attention to the welfare of another is a reliable marker of emotional health. While we all are, to some extent, self-absorbed—particularly when we struggle with personal challenges—the intensity and duration are revealing. Almost anyone can be warm, kind, and generous when he is in a positive mood. However, a true indicator of emotional health is when a person can respond to the needs of another with care and patience even while in a low emotional state or under physical distress.

A person who is not self-centered feels humility and a connection to others. The wall of *I am me and he is he* is broken down, and where there is no ego, there is connection, a bond. For this reason we naturally feel empathy more easily for children, the elderly, the sick, or even animals, because we see their vulnerability via their ego-free appearance. They look the part. We experience this in our own lives in different ways, to different degrees. A person bangs into us on a busy street and we turn around, annoyed, only to find that he's blind or otherwise handicapped and is simply trying to get past us. We see his limitation, we feel for him—our "heart goes out to him"—and our anger dissipates. Or maybe a coworker spills coffee on your desk and dashes away. You're about to walk into her office and pounce, only to learn that her child is sick in the hosptial. Anger cannot exist where there is no separation, no "I" to get in the way, but when we are self-focused, the ego cuts the cord. Fundamentally, anger is a disconnection—to avoid pain, to inflict pain.

To be a part of someone's life we need to create a space for that person. If one is too self-absorbed, there is no room for anyone else, and such a person is trapped in the tomb of his own suffering because his capacity to connect with others is strained, if not altogether severed. Physical isolation—or even simply being ignored—is painful. In fact, studies show that feeling alone or experiencing loneliness, more than any other factor, causes extreme stress and an overall weakening of the immune system. The pain of isolation is not just a metaphor. Functional magnetic resonance imaging (fMRI) scans reveal that two areas of the brain where we process physical pain—the *dorsal anterior cingulate cortex* and the *anterior insula*—become activated when we experience feelings of social rejection.[3] The lower the self-esteem, the weaker the connection to our true selves—the soul—and to the true selves of others—as such, our ability to give love and to receive love erodes. We suffer. Our relationships suffer. Everyone suffers.

SMOKE AND MIRRORS

We should note that people often mistake confidence for self-esteem, but the two are quite different. Confidence is how effective we feel within a specific area or situation, while self-esteem is defined as how much we recognize our inherent worth and feel deserving of happiness and good fortune. Self-esteem is shaped by the quality of our choices rather than by the assets at our disposal. A person who attempts to fortify his self-image by taking pride in a specific trait may exhibit signs of high self-esteem to the untrained eye, but, in fact, such an individual often suffers from low self-esteem, because all he has is an inflated ego.

When a person suffers from very low self-esteem, it doesn't matter how accomplished he appears, he depends on everyone and everything to boost his faltering self-image. The research is clear: A person's inflated sense of self does not derive from self-esteem, but from self-loathing.[4] Don't fall into the trap of believing that a person with an inflated ego likes himself; ego and self-esteem are inversely related. No matter how much a person appears to be happy with himself, if he is egocentric, that person suffers with feelings of inferiority. This statement is not conjecture, but a law of human nature; it is psychological math.[5]

4

Step Right Up and Choose Your Reality

Each circumstance we encounter is like a blank book until we write the script with our thoughts. For instance, when someone acts rudely toward us, it doesn't *mean* anything. This person's words or deeds *cause* us to feel bad about ourselves because of *our* self-image. What does his opinion really have to do with our self-worth? Nothing. But that's just what the ego does—it makes everything about us. The greater our self-esteem, the less quick we are to take offense because when we love ourselves, (a) we don't assume that someone's actions mean he doesn't respect us; and (b) even if we do come to that conclusion, we aren't angered, because we don't *need* his respect in order to respect ourselves.

We often unconsciously evaluate a situation to determine how personally we should take it and thus how offended we should feel. For example, a car cuts us off on the road, and we are curious to see what the driver looks like. Why? Based on the driver's appearance, we try to determine if the action was deliberate. An elderly man, wearing a gray fedora and driving a 1983 Oldsmobile would not enrage us as much as a young man smoking a cigarette with music blaring from his car's open windows. Most of us would assume that the older gentleman simply didn't see our car while the young man *did it to us* on purpose, because he doesn't respect us and doesn't care. Do you appreciate the absurdity of this? We get cut off on the road, and then we speed up to see what the offending driver looks like so we can decide how angry we should become.

Whatever the situation or circumstance—the question we ask ourselves is always the same: *What does this mean?* That's what anger comes down to; it's not only that you take it personally. Rather, it's the belief that, *This person treated me this way* because *there's something wrong with me*—something broken or flawed. As we discussed in Chapter 2, if you don't love and respect yourself, then you can't imagine why anyone else would have positive feelings toward you. *I don't like me, so you must not like me.* We connect the dots of someone else's behavior to arrive at a place of hurt. We assume that the person has treated us this way because, *They know the truth.* This frightful thought makes us question our self-worth: *Maybe I deserve this.*

We often experience more pain when we feel disrespected by a smart, wealthy, or attractive person. Via the ego, we believe that this individual has more value, and so his treatment of us is of greater significance. Indeed, our relationship to the person also shapes the impact. If a crazed person starts screaming at us, we will likely be minimally affected by the encounter—but what if it's a close friend, a respected colleague, or a loved one? Why are we more inclined to feel hurt and prone to become angry? Because this person knows us inside and out—the good, the bad, and the ugly. This can cause us to more easily question our self-worth. *This person really knows me. Maybe there's something to it?*

The flaw in this thinking is a corrupted correlation between a person's knowledge of us and his treatment of us. Just because someone knows you well, it doesn't make him healthy. If a person has one hundred percent self-esteem, speaking theoretically, he would approach the entire world with love and respect. When conversing with a rude person, for example, he would be filled with empathy. His singular thought would be, *How much pain must this person be in to treat someone as wonderful as me so poorly?* Again, we can only give what we have. We give love. We give respect. How someone behaves toward you is reflection of his own feelings of self-worth and has nothing to do with your intrinsic worth—unless you (the ego) decide to make it about you.

Likewise, when you're in a good mood—brimming with transitory feelings of confidence and control—does it mean that others are suddenly worthier of your respect and kindness? No one has changed but you. As our mood sours, we become emotionally stingy and give respect to those we need. We are not really giving anything, though, but rather taking masquerading as giving.

IT'S NOT ME, IT'S YOU

In the previous chapter, we explained that when we know a person's limitations, animosity is diffused because once we see their vulnerability and fragility, we don't make his problem our problem. And while the more arrogant a person appears to be on the outside, the more weak and helpless he feels on the inside, it is we who determine whether we will see beyond the façade. Once our is ego deployed, we become fearful—the knee jerk conclusion is, *How dare he!*—and the fuse is lit. If, however, we are primed to observe the basis for his behavior—his feelings of inadequacy and insecurity—then we remain anger free. If not filled with empathy, than at least with pity. As long as we are alert to the pain of the other person, the entire interaction is automatically reframed and we will not *feel* pained because we will not *be* in pain. But the moment we become self-focused we will draw the inevitable conclusion that this treatment is because we are less— rather than he feels less—and that's scary. That's painful.

It's not the situation that determines how you feel but the meaning that we attach to it, and that meaning is always based on one thing: how we feel about ourselves. There is an event and an emotional response, but in between those is an intellectual process where we assign a meaning to what is happening. The instant you choose to take it personally—yes, it's a choice—you'll be fighting against your nature. Imagine that you're at a party and someone starts screaming at you for being a lying, no-good thief and hurls a string of accusations at you. The music stops and the crowd stares. You're feeling mortified until . . . he calls you by the wrong name. Realizing that this is a case of mistaken identity and everyone now knows it, you move from humiliation to relief as your focus shifts from yourself to this poor guy and how embarrassed he's going to be the moment he learns the truth. In all interactions, if your ego is out of the way, then you know that, "He's got the wrong person." It's not you. Unless you make it about you. While it's true that he may see you as less, that doesn't *make* you less— but if you feel less, then it does make you angry.

THE STORY WE SELL OURSELVES

When someone close to us—our spouse, for example—does something we don't like, the behavior itself is one thing, but that is *not* what drives our anger. Rather, it is the belief that our spouse's behavior *means* that he or she doesn't love us enough, really care about us enough, or have enough respect for us. Let's parse out the *what* from the *why* to see how our ego so easily leads us astray.

If you got upset with your spouse, who then apologized profusely, asked for forgiveness, and then did everything that he could to make it up to you, would you have a harder time maintaining the anger? Understandably, you would still object to the behavior, but should your spouse take full responsibility and convey that his failings are not due to a lack of love or appreciation for you, anger is harder to sustain. The reality has not changed, but the meaning that you assigned to the behavior has, and that changes how you feel about the behavior. Certainly, we can see how this may apply to minor lapses or offenses, but I suspect we can conjure up a scenario or two that might have us fuming mad at the situation itself—ego or no ego. In Part IV, we will explore more deeply how to uproot anger even in the case of a highly significant event or severe breach of trust.

But, still on this subject, let's assume that our spouse does *not* have respect for us. Fine. Again, we ask ourselves a single question: *What does this mean?* It may mean that our spouse lacks self-esteem and thus cannot effectively give and receive love and respect. It may mean that we have to look in the mirror at our own conduct and ask ourselves, *Have I been kind and loving to my spouse? Has my behavior played a role in his attitude toward me?* Whatever conclusion we draw, the one that is never accurate is the ego-based: *I deserve this because there is something wrong with me.* Our conduct may have been wrong, but this does not mean that we are bad and undeserving of love and happiness. If we believe this to be true at a conscious level, then we live out our lives in victim mode, for this is the treatment that we deserve. If we harbor this belief unconsciously then we become enraged at every perceived or genuine lack of respect. Moreover, we will be looking for signs that we are not worthy of love and respect. If we don't find them, we will convince ourselves that we have, by reading into things and jumping to conclusions. This is, in fact, at the core of jealous thinking: *I am not worthy of you, so you must not be faithful to me.* If this is my belief, then I become hyper-tuned-in to anything that will fortify my position, and I will "see" what I need to in order to prove myself right. I will connect dots to complete the narrative so that it tells my story.

ANGER: THE FINE PRINT

The intricacies of anger are often simplified to the point of being incomplete. To say that we become angry because we are scared or in pain is like saying that a lamp works because the light switch is flipped on—true enough, but the underlying connection, electricity, is left out of the equation. Pain in and of itself does not lead to anger. Neither does fear. Mountain climbing and crossword puzzles can be grueling and excruciating. A roller coaster or horror movie can be terrifying. And yet, these can also be exhilarating and enjoyable. However, an eighteen-wheeler veering into your lane, your small child running into the street, a careless person banging into you at work, or your boss yelling at you may very well provoke anger. What is the difference in these scenarios?: control.

What activates anger is an emotional or physical pain that we cannot control. Fear comes into play because fear itself is emotionally painful, with fear of the unknown—which carries a complete lack of control—having the potential to bring the greatest pain. Opposite sides of the same coin: unpredictable or uncontrollable pain brings fear, and fear that we cannot predict or control is painful. Since it is the ego that seeks control, even emotional pain in proper context (widened, ego-free perspective) is diluted. A close friend receives tragic news and makes a scene in a public place, but feelings of embarrassment take a backseat to empathy over their sorrow. A loved one lashes out at us in anger because we caused him hurt, but rather than feel rejected, we feel for him and seek to allay his fears.

THE SHAME GAME

Human beings experience two primary emotions: love (which is soul-based) and fear (which is ego-based). All positive emotions stem from love, and all negative emotions stem from fear; the fear of isolation, because we are unfit to be loved. Which brings us to *shame*. Shame is our conscience, the voice of the soul that says *I am less because of my actions*; it is the painful belief that our behavior makes us unworthy of love and undeserving of acceptance—and by extension, all that we love is neither safe nor secure. This pain of legitimate shame is to alert us that we have fallen below our potential. In accepting responsibility, we not only cancel the emotional debt but we receive the benefit of enhanced self-esteem; and with it, the capacity to love and to be loved as well as a host of emotional dividends including trust in our future welfare (see Chapter 11 for elaboration). However, when we are confronted by either circumstance or conscience, and deny accountability, we will to varying degrees and levels of consciousness acquire a stain of shame—because we cannot lie to our deepest selves. (Part IV shows the process to free ourselves from shame and restore our feelings of self-worth to pristine condition.)

Therein lies the origin of anger: As the ego compensates for feelings of unresolved shame, we experience a counterfeit shame: *I am less if **you** think I am less.*[1] Feeling rejected in any way (embarrassed, criticized, unwanted, mocked, and the like) is excruciatingly painful and intensely feared because it feels to us (the ego, the false self) like genuine shame. The egocentric psyche translates any rejection to mean that *I am inadequate. I will not be safe and accepted because I am unworthy of love and undeserving of good.* A further aberration explains misplaced shame, which is rooted in the corrupted belief that says: *I am responsible for the behavior of others.* In which case, we are never blameless for whatever is done to us, because we are a coconspirator—both victim and abuser. In Chapter 14 we explain that because children are egocentric by nature, it is normal for them to ascribe a failure within themselves as the reason behind the behavior of others. Therefore, if we, as children, grew up believing that we were never good enough to merit our parent's love and approval, or we are mistreated, held to unrealistic expectations, or forced to assume responsibilities that weren't ours, shame—the feeling that we have failed, fallen below our potential, is imprinted. We all transition to adulthood having absorbed some shame (which is why we feel ashamed for inherent flaws and faults, which we neither caused nor contributed to—and of course, that we all have); and the more damaging the childhood, the greater the ego and accompanying shame.

The ego is on the lookout for any situation that calls into question our worth, fearful that we are not lovable and may be rejected. Hence, the opposite of control—feeling vulnerable or even being stared at, let alone being disrespected or ridiculed, can send the egocentric psyche into overdrive. It becomes clear then why relationships, particularly with those closest to us, can result in unrelenting anger—it sets off so many emotional triggers. Take a simple scenario: a child does not listen to a parent.

- Guilt (Maybe I've done a poor job parenting.)
- Disrespect (How dare he not listen to me!)
- Rejection (He doesn't love me.)
- Embarrassment (If others are around, *what do they think of me?*)
- Fear (What's going to become of him? What will become of our relationship?)
- Injustice (After all I've done for him.)

Whenever there is a threat to our emotional (or physical) selves, the lower our self-esteem, in general—and how much the uncomfortable truth hits a raw nerve and affects our self-image, in particular—the more fearful we become of feeling that pain; as a result, our need to exert control surges. Authentic control is actuated when we rise above our nature and exercise self-control, thus rendering the fear/pain mechanism inert. Anger is the illusion of control because physiologically, the release of the neurotransmitter noradrenaline and the hormone adrenaline increases awareness, energy, and strength. Emotionally, anger redirects our attention away from the fear/pain, which also mimics the sensation that we have seized control. The reality, of course, is that we spiral out of control and become weaker with each intense, anger-driven thought or action. Our personality will dictate how our anger manifests (explained further in Chapter 21) and mirrors the *fight-or-flight* response to a physical threat.

- Assertive aggressive (*fight*): We come out fighting attempting to control the situation overtly.
- Passive aggressive (*flight*): Anger leaks out in more subtle ways. Unable to confront directly, we seek control stealthily.
- Surrender or Suppression (*flight*): We are unable to consciously acknowledge our anger, so we control it by either (a) telling ourselves that we are not worthy of asserting ourselves or (b) suppressing our emotions and telling ourselves that we are not angered to begin with.
- Immobilization (*freeze*): Feeling powerless, we close down to insulate ourselves from the pain. I can avoid. I can shut out the world. I will be safe. I will be in control.

The *fight-or-flight* response is a physiological reaction to a perceived threat, and is triggered whether the danger is real or imagined. For example, whether we see a bear in the woods or believe that we see one, the response is the same: The sympathetic nervous system activates the adrenal gland, which releases adrenaline, noradrenaline, and cortisol into the bloodstream and reroutes the threat from the prefrontal cortex (the thinking brain) to the amygdala (the fear and anxiety response center). The moment, however, that we realize that there is no bear, the response disengages—because the danger no longer exists. Likewise, becoming aware that we are not experiencing shame, but its counterfeit, neutralizes the threat. We have nothing to fear and no need to exert control because the pain is not real. We are not in danger. We are already safe.[2]

PART II

THE COST OF LIVING, THE PRICE OF ESCAPING

5
Why Smart People Do Dumb Things

A man known in medical literature as Elliot became a famous figure in brain research when he suffered damage to the frontal lobes of his brain as the result of a tumor. Although he enjoyed a superior IQ, he would become lost in triviality and foolish pursuits. After giving Elliot a battery of tests, his physician, leading scientist Dr. Antonio Damasio, realized that the man was incapable of emotional expression. Although intellectually he could weigh the pros and cons of any decision, when it came time to actually decide, he was completely lost. Damasio states, "His decision-making landscape was hopelessly flat."[1] In his book *Descartes' Error*, Damasio describes trying to set up an appointment with Elliot:

> I suggested two alternative dates, both in the coming month and just a few days apart from each other. The patient pulled out his appointment book and began consulting the calendar. The behavior that ensued, which was witnessed by several investigators, was remarkable. For the better part of a half hour, the patient enumerated reasons for and against each of the two dates: previous engagements, proximity to other engagements, possible meteorological conditions, virtually anything that one could think about

concerning a simple date. [He was] walking us through a tiresome cost-benefit analysis, an endless outlining and fruitless comparison of options and possible consequences. It took enormous discipline to listen to all of this without pounding on the table and telling him to stop.[2]

Indeed, it did stop. All it took was for Damasio to interrupt the man's deliberations and assign him a date and a time to return. Without hesitating, the patient said, "That's fine," and went on his way.

VULCANS NEED NOT APPLY

When we have no drive to mobilize our passion, nothing reinforces the intellectual process that moves us in one direction or the other. This is one primary function that emotions serve: to energize our behavior and motivate us to take action. We need emotions, but when we lead with our feelings, our intellect then fortifies a distorted conclusion. To choose wisely, we must first see clearly through the lens of the intellect and afterward align our emotions— preferably, positive ones. A person is always better off identifying with the love of the virtue for which he is fighting than acting out of anger, which is always ego-based. Meaning that focusing on our passion for what is right, rather than on our disdain for what is wrong, will help us to see more clearly and to act more responsibly because we are not blinded by outrage. This is not a pacifist approach but one that allows for an optimum response. No one ever walked away from an argument and thought, *I wish I had gotten angrier, I would have been able to handle myself so much better.*

Later in the chapter, we will see how anger robs us of our intelligence—the faculty to process reality—but first we will see how it distorts our ability to *see* clearly. Wisdom is a function of both intellectual and emotional clarity. To the degree that our ego is engaged, we unconsciously distort (or consciously ignore) reality and gravitate toward the less-responsible choice. Therefore, in any given situation, it's quite possible for a smart person to make an astonishingly poor decision while his less-intelligent counterpart will make the wiser, more prudent choice.

Self-esteem and emotional health (aka wisdom, which is synonymous with an expanded perspective) go hand in hand. Intelligence, however, is largely unrelated to either self-esteem or emotional well-being. An overweight diabetic with low self-esteem knows she shouldn't eat chocolate cake for dinner, but she eats it anyway. Her low self-esteem is directing the choice she makes. In that moment, she's more interested in the chocolate cake than in her physical health. The hallmark of emotional maturity is the ability to delay gratification—to bear some pain now (or to give up a lower-level pleasure) in exchange for a greater pleasure later (or to avoid a small pain from becoming a bigger pain).

Intelligence does not make a person rational. Intelligence can only put us in the driver's seat with a map in hand. Wisdom opens our eyes to see what we wish would not exist; to accept with grace; and to respond with clarity and confidence.

SELF-ESTEEM AND DELAYING GRATIFICATION
Self-esteem stimulates the desire to invest in ourselves and provides the energy for self-discipline. When our self-esteem is low,

our interest and attention shift from long-term to immediate gratification—if it feels good, do it, regardless of the consequences. The most appealing choice will be the one that satisfies our immediate urges. We resemble the child who would rather have one lollipop now than five lollipops tomorrow. Five lollipops, of course, is the better bargain, but the child doesn't think about that. His focus is short-term, shallow, and narrow. He is occupied with the here and now, often forsaking his long-term self-interest—let alone the bigger picture or, even more so, the needs of others.

It is significant to note the landmark experiment dubbed "the marshmallow test," which looked into the ability of children to delay gratification, and the resulting long-term correlation and consequences. Conducted at Stanford University, researchers gave a marshmallow to each child participating in the experiment with the following offer: Either eat this one marshmallow right away, or wait a short while and receive an additional marshmallow. The researcher then left the room, and the child was alone with a marshmallow in front of him. In follow-ups a decade later, the children who delayed their gratification were more successful both academically and socially.[3] Analysis concluded that they reported fewer pathological symptoms (including obsessive-compulsive patterns, depression, anxiety, hostile anger, phobic anxiety, paranoid ideation, and psychoticism) and exhibited higher self-acceptance and self-esteem.

ANGRY PEOPLE BEHAVE STUPIDLY

Research finds self-regulation failure is central to nearly all the personal and social problems that currently plague the modern, developed world. These problems include drug addiction and abuse, alcoholism, smoking, crime and violence, underachievement in schools, gambling, personal debt and credit card abuse, lack of financial savings, anger, and hostility.[4]

Among the most important triggers of self-regulation failure (in plain English, what makes us lose self-control and give in to our impulses) is anger.[5] The following excerpt from a benchmark research paper summarizes the unsurprising range of self-destructive behaviors that anger spawns.[6]

When people become upset they sometimes act aggressively,[7] spend too much money,[8] engage in risky behavior,[9] comfort with alcohol, drugs or food, and fail to pursue important life goals.[10] Anger is related to relapse for a number of addictive behaviors, such as alcoholism, gambling and drug addiction;[11] and increased eating by chronic dieters[12] and greater smoking intensity by smokers.[13]

Anger releases a stress hormone called cortisol. Long-term elevated cortisol levels have a detrimental effect on us, both physically and mentally. Specifically, cortisol damages cells in the hippocampus and results in impaired learning. In the short term, cortisol interferes with our ability to think and process information. Or, to put it another way, getting angry actually makes us dumb. Biochemically, anger, as we know, initiates the fight-or-flight response and the production of adrenaline, which reroutes blood flow away from the brain, and with it oxygen, which further muddles our thinking.

Wisdom is one of the most powerful by-products of emotional

health, and it gives us the capacity and fortitude to see the situation objectively and then respond calmly and logically, rather than allowing anger to corrupt our observation, assessment, judgment, and conduct.

6
A Fight to the Death

Even the healthiest among us are not immune to being swayed by our emotions. We often require little convincing to do what we feel like doing, and we frequently act against flawless logic when we find it convenient or comfortable. It's not about reason and rationale, it's about emotion and desire. With cigarette warnings of severe consequences in plain view, tens of millions of people still smoke. An avalanche of literature on the hazards of obesity and the importance of exercise is ignored by 67 percent of the population, who remain overweight or obese. Hundreds of studies bring us to near-universal agreement that money doesn't buy happiness, yet 55 percent of the adult population is in debt—trying to buy their way into happiness. What does logic have to do with it?

As self-esteem fades and the ego's noose tightens, our entire decision-making system falls prey to corruption. We descend from thinking to feeling and too often respond by shooting first and asking questions later. We become stuck in a perpetual cycle of bad decisions, and then we feel further compelled to justify our previous actions, regardless of the consequences. We eat food that we don't want because we ordered it. We read a book that we don't want to read because we walked all the way to the library in the rain to borrow it. Ralph Waldo Emerson poetically condensed the folly of this mind-set: "A foolish consistency is the hobgoblin of little minds."[1]

Growth is internalized when we tell ourselves, *I was wrong, and now I will do what is right*. We must be able to accept that we have been doing something that never made sense—or no longer does—instead of hiding behind a wall of explanations and rationalizations. Those whose egos reign lack self-esteem and can't afford to question their own judgment, worth, or intelligence. Justification then binds them to the past and drags their mistakes into the future.[2]

TWO WRONGS DON'T MAKE A RIGHT

As hard as it may be to admit defeat and throw in the towel, investing additional resources in a pursuit or project that's going nowhere is certainly not productive. We need to cut our losses and channel our energy into more constructive options, but the ego forces us forward—clinging tight to false or damaging beliefs and behaviors, even when they're hurting us. *Loss aversion* refers to our ego's tendency to lean toward avoiding loss, rather than acquiring gains. It's not just that we can't stand losing; we can't stand even the *possibility* of losing, admitting defeat.

Why do rational people sometimes make irrational decisions? Why do we willingly throw good money after bad? As any master stock trader will advise, we start losing money the second we allow our emotions to influence our trading decisions. When investors put on blinders, ignore empirical evidence, and dedicate themselves to recovering as much of their loss as possible, we say they're "chasing a loss." It's one thing to do this with a stock, but it's quite another to do this with our lives.

Our commitment to stubborn persistence tends to become

stronger once we have invested time, money, or energy into something—whether it's a tumbling stock, a doomed relationship, or a dead-end job. If we make a hopeless investment, it's easy to succumb to the sunk-cost fallacy: *I can't quit now because I'll lose everything I've already invested!* This is true, of course, but it's irrelevant to whether we should continue to invest. Everything we have already invested *is* lost. We can't do anything to change that. Misguided commitment is nothing more than a delay tactic, which is the toxic offspring of denial—a refusal to accept what is.

RIGHT TO THE END

Even after the facts become obvious, an intelligent but ego-oriented person might stay the course of a bad decision and persist in outright self-destructive behavior. Unable to emerge victorious, the ego shrewdly switches tactics and declares us to be a casualty of fate, circumstance, or others' cruel conniving, to avoid taking responsibility for our actions and our lives. We become locked into these patterns and too often manipulate events to unfold in accordance with our expectations. It's how we need the world to be. Being right becomes more of an emotional priority than doing what is right. We act against our own best interests because, unconsciously, we need to prove to ourselves and to others that we are victims. In this way, we perpetuate our own misery. We align the entirety of our lives to accommodate *our story*.

Renowned psychologist Dr. Nathaniel Branden wrote about a woman he once treated who grew up thinking she was "bad" and undeserving of kindness, respect, or happiness. Predictably, she married a man who "knew" he was unlovable and felt consumed by self-hatred. He protected himself by acting cruelly toward others before they could be cruel to him. She didn't complain about his abuse because she "knew" that abuse was her destiny. He wasn't surprised by her increasing withdrawal and remoteness from him, because he "knew" no one could ever love him. They endured twenty years of torture together, proving how right they were about themselves and about life.[3]

When we suffer from low self-esteem, we're often afraid that something bad will happen to us after something good occurs in our lives. When fortune unexpectedly smiles on us, we feel anxious because of our sense of unworthiness. To alleviate our emotional tension, we might even sabotage our success so that we can fulfill our personal prophecy: The world is as we predicted. We feel secure because our beliefs—no matter how damaging and distorted—have been reaffirmed. We will be right, even if it kills us.

7
Reality Isn't Going Anywhere

All roads out of reality lead to the Land of Suffering. Avoidance is not coping. It's crashing in slow motion. It's easier, too, for us to ignore reality than it used to be. In days of old, we tended to make better choices because the consequences of our poor judgments were immediate and trickier to conceal. Today, we have a "buy now, pay later" mentality. Suffering indigestion because we ate more than our body can metabolize? Take an antacid. Lactose intolerant? Take Lactaid. If we ingest too much of the wrong thing, don't worry. There are laxatives for constipation. Antidiarrheal for diarrhea. Aspirin for headaches. And calcium carbonate hangover prevention supplements to nip those hangovers in the bud.

Interest may be deferred, but that balloon payment will come due sooner or later. This mentality is nicely captured in an old joke: A man jumps from the top of a twenty-story building, and as he falls to the ground, a woman at the tenth floor sees him from her window and shouts, "How's it going?" The man replies, "So far, so good." Making things more problematic is that we have far more means of escapism at our disposal, allowing us to blithely ignore our reality. Technology—arguably, an addiction in itself—has become a popular enabler, the new Great Escape. Computers, televisions, smart phones . . . everywhere we turn, we find convenient vehicles for mindless distraction. Instant shrink-wrapped entertainment offers escape into other worlds, a never-ending labyrinth of video games, movies, TV shows, blogs, and forums where we can dissociate from the pain du jour. We need to be distracted, to be taken away from ourselves. The uncomfortable noise of self-reflection muted, and the volume of illusion turned way up.

The addictive nature of technology magnifies not just the emotional lure, but the physiological pull. The inevitable multitasking leads to overstimulation, and creates "a dopamine-addiction feedback loop, effectively rewarding the brain for losing focus and for constantly searching for external stimulation."[1] These effects contribute to impaired emotional processing, lack of concentration, high stress and anxiety levels, and impaired decision making.[2]

MEANING = PLEASURE

As life becomes increasingly more comfortable, we've fallen out of the habit of exerting ourselves. We've come to believe that comfort is the path to happiness. Perhaps even more damaging is the notion that comfort *is* happiness. The idea of sacrificing our creature comforts to pursue our goals and dreams has become foreign to our thinking. In our minds, life should be easy.

Lying on the couch and watching TV is undoubtedly comfortable, but hardly meaningful, and so, by definition, offers no genuine pleasure and certainly no fulfillment. To be more precise, the feeling is not really pleasure at all, but mere comfort, which is the avoidance of pain. If we seek to avoid the pain, though, of legitimate challenges, then we are, in essence, avoiding life, and rather than minimizing pain and maximizing pleasure, we will maximize suffering and live exceedingly unfulfilled lives.

How would you feel if someone pulled a few strings to get you a great job? You would probably feel pretty good. How might you feel if you found out, after thirty years on the job, that everything was fake; that you had pushed buttons not attached to any working machine, and your phone calls had been answered by actors who were merely playing along? In fact, you were wildly successful at your job, but none of it was real. Most people would be devastated—but why? The answer is simple: Your work was not real and had no meaning, therefore was not pleasurable. So goes meaning, so goes pleasure.

The more engaged we are in life and the pursuit of meaningful goals, the greater our pleasure and ultimate sense of satisfaction. Do we really want to live superficial, comfortable lives that lack meaning? No matter how much effort we expend, our satisfaction dissipates if the objective is not purposeful. Being comfortable and having fun are not enough. Our soul gnaws at us not just to do more, but to *become* something more. Make no mistake, the pursuit of ego-oriented objectives—those that bring money, power, and fame as a means unto themselves—takes us out of reality as completely and as quickly as the pursuit of amusement and recreation unto themselves. Viktor Frankl described this as "an unheard cry for meaning," and Freud writes, "It is impossible to escape the impression that people commonly use false standards of measurement—that they seek power, success and wealth for themselves and admire them in others, and that they underestimate what is of true value in life."

CHASING COMFORT = PAIN

Our fruitless attempts to hide from life not only deny us pleasure, but also move us into the waiting arms of emotional disease, because in the attempt to bypass pain, we short-circuit our mental health. Research shows that the more modern a society, the higher its rate of depression.[3] Technology leaves idle hands and frees up many hours each day. With this freedom, we can fill our lives with either time well spent or time misused, abused, or utterly wasted.[4]

Unsurprisingly, people without work are more likely to suffer psychological trouble and stress-related illnesses such as diabetes, heart disease, and stroke. They also have diminished life expectancy.[5] In fact, even at work, a person can literally be bored to death. In a UK study, 7,500 London civil servants ages 35 to 55 filled out a simple questionnaire in which they were asked if they had felt bored at work during the previous month. The researchers followed up to determine how many of the participants had died after approximately ten years. Workers who reported they had been "very bored" were two and a half times more likely to have died of a heart-related ailment than were those who had said they were "not bored."[6]

Depression is often described as a taste of death. When we die, our soul—the real us—separates from the body. A person who doesn't grow and move forward in life will force a rift between the body and the soul—the very experience of death itself.[7] We feel this lack of harmony as depression. Our soul aches to grow, and stagnation feels like death because it is—a spiritual death. The accompanying feeling of futility—that what we do doesn't matter—leads to the inevitable, excruciating conclusion that we don't matter.

Our soul is rigged to revolt against negligence and indifference, and the system will faithfully keep dishing out new symptoms—both emotional and physical—to remind us that we exist in this world for a reason. Every soul has a distinct mission, infused with its own spiritual DNA. It longs to rise from the masses and to light up creation by unleashing its unique spark of the Infinite. For this reason, we feel more distraught to learn of the injury or the death of a young person than we do of an elderly person. Loss of life is unequivocally sad, but we find the loss of potential particularly heartbreaking. The wider the gap between potential and actualization, the sadder it seems. Likewise, the extent to which we fall short of our own potential, the greater the waste and the more frustration and shame we experience.

NO ESCAPE FROM REALITY

Living in reality is more than just choosing between "right" and "wrong." In a larger sense, it is a choice between life and death. Choosing responsibly means engaging life, rather than neglecting life and dying, ever so slowly.

HAMLET: ACT 3, SCENE 1

To be or not to be, that is the question.
Whether 'tis nobler in the mind to suffer
The slings and arrows of outrageous fortune,
Or to take arms against a sea of troubles,
And by opposing, end them? To die: to sleep;
No more; and by a sleep to say we end
The heart-ache and the thousand natural shocks . . .

Hamlet speaks of the pain and distress that permeate human existence. He contemplates his choices: Either I endure the trials of life, or I end it with suicide. And by suicide, we don't mean one tormented act to end it all but, rather, the discrete death of escapism. That is the challenge we confront each day. Will we rise to meet life head-on or turn away and sink into the deceptive comfort of a counterfeit existence?

Emotional health demands allegiance to reality. Any time we move away from the swift current of life, we become less stable because we disconnect from truth. Should we move too far into our own world, even an insignificant event shifts our fertile imagination into overdrive, consuming us with mushrooming fear and anxiety. Our lives overfill with tragedies that never happen.

Paradoxically, the more neurotic a person is, the more he believes in his ability to see, know, and predict the world around him. In actuality, he is less able to recognize cause-and-effect relationships. To compensate for his impairment, to feel some sense of control, he creates his own associations between action and consequence. Naturally, this compounds his neurosis, because when the inevitable breach occurs, he retreats deeper into his assumptions.[8] Superstition is nothing but a diluted form of paranoia—the desire to make connections where none exist. All of reality is an undifferentiated facet of the whole, so patterns and connections are everywhere, but when a person can't see beyond himself, the soul's desire to make connections is supplanted by the ego's own self-oriented correlations. Because the individual can't find meaning, he invents it.

Further compounding our emotional strain is mistaking affliction for accomplishment. Sometimes we seek distress, rather than success, and tell ourselves that *pain equals progress*. So we might unconsciously create obstacles to give ourselves the illusion of forward movement. Here's an example of a common tactic: The file that we absolutely can't afford to lose, our cellular phone, our vehicle registration—just about everything and anything that we can misplace, we will misplace. Essentially, we manufacture a challenge in a controlled environment that, once overcome, gives us a sense of excitement and accomplishment. It is a feeble attempt to feel the rush of life without making the effort of living. In some instances, we devise these challenges because, unconsciously, we *want* to inconvenience ourselves. Feelings of guilt and self-recrimination cause us to inflict harm on ourselves—the very epitome of self-destruction.

THE ADRENALINE JUNKIE CONNECTION

Sometimes people engage in high-risk behavior to feel alive. Even though they may be tremendously successful by societal standards, there is a lacking on the inside, a disconnect from the soul that makes them feel half-dead. They risk death for the jolt—the adrenaline rush—so that they can, at least in the moment, feel alive. Adrenaline, as noted earlier, is a stimulating hormone naturally released by the brain in response to extreme stress or anxiety. Its purpose is to send a surge of awareness and strength during a dangerous situation or crisis and creates a temporary natural high, elevated senses, and a feeling of power and control. (Neurotransmitters, such as endorphins and dopamine are also released, and they add to the experience.) What makes this fact most relevant is that intense anger triggers the fight-or-flight response and produces a similar sense of euphoria. Hence, the more one lives in accord with the soul, the less he needs the drug of anger to make him *feel alive.*

Imagine a thimble and bucket each filled with a liquid. The

thimble feels as full as the bucket. Can we say that the bucket is fuller than the thimble? In relative terms, the bucket has more liquid; in absolute terms, they are each full. The same can be said for human beings. Some people are miserable, even though by all accounts they make good choices. This is because we each stand on a never-ending ladder of attainment, whose starting point is irrelevant. We might be capable of climbing easily, but we choose to be complacent and climb only a few rungs at our leisure. We can measure our genuine progress—and therefore our self-esteem and emotional health—only by looking at our effort in relation to our ability. Maslow succinctly summarizes this point: "If you plan on being anything less than you are capable of being, you will probably be unhappy and angry all of the days of your life."[9]

8
The Meaning of Pleasure, the Pleasure of Meaning

Living a life with meaning not only brings pleasure and bolsters our emotional, spiritual, and physical health, but it also results in less suffering. That's not to say that difficulties don't come or that people who endure misfortune or trauma in any way bring it upon themselves. Such painful circumstances are too often beyond our finite understanding, and are not necessarily the result of our actions. Yet pain is not the same as suffering. Suffering is the emotional consequence of our choices.

How we feel about ourselves determines how long pain lingers and whether it morphs into suffering. The equation is simple: Being self-centered = suffering. This explains why an emotionally immature person, one with low self-esteem (or a child, perhaps), becomes agitated over every little thing that goes wrong. In fact, the attributes of someone with a narrow perspective can be characterized as childlike. Small children are egocentric beings. They react to their environment with sudden tantrums, mindless exuberance, wild mood swings, and an absolute, black-and-white view of events. They are quick to misread or misinterpret others' behavior, and they overreact to perceived insults, slights, and criticism.

Without the emotional shock absorber of perspective, we feel only pain—and pain that persists is suffering. That's because perspective provides context, and context allows us to more easily attach significance and meaning to challenges. We can see how seemingly disparate facets integrate into a larger whole, and each new piece of the puzzle that we identify helps clarify and define what we already know. Imagine the wings of a butterfly magnified a thousand times. Being so close to it, we can't tell what it is, what it does, or why it exists. It's necessary to take a step back to see what it really is. Then its design, details, and meaning become clear. The wings are part of a larger organism. Everything begins to make sense when we have perspective.

Research on physical pain management also shows us that pain severity depends on the context in which the pain occurs. The pain threshold—someone's ability to bear pain—increases as the person better understands the body's healing process and the role of pain in healing. This explains why people who suffer from major depression have a lower pain threshold.[1] As an individual becomes increasingly focused on himself, he loses perspective, then context, and then meaning. He is left with only pain, and much of life—living itself—becomes hard.

When we buy a gift for a loved one, we can't wait to give it, to see the pleasure it brings. We can work tirelessly for someone we care about or for a cause we believe in and not feel the pain—and perhaps experience great joy—because our focus is on the larger, meaningful objective. Hours fly by, and we don't realize it. Similarly, when we love ourselves, we can invest in our long-term satisfaction and well-being with maximum effort and minimal pain. Even though we expend a great deal of energy, self-esteem taps us into the Infinite, a limitless source. How we feel about our-selves determines whether we are focused on the pleasure or on the pain—and defines the entirety of the experience.

WHAT DOESN'T BREAK US

We all know people who led charmed lives, with every advan-tage during their youth and upbringing, but later made a succes-sion of stunningly irresponsible choices that dragged them down a path of misery. We are equally mindful of those who have been dealt one challenge after another yet soared above even the most daunting heartaches, embracing their futures with steadfast cour-age and optimism.

A range of ceaseless heartaches and anguish—imprisonment, betrayal, treachery, and murder—awaited every great figure in the Bible without exception: Adam, Noah, Sarah, Rachel, Leah, Jo-seph, Moses, Aaron, King David, King Solomon—and the list goes on. Who could argue that the lives of these Bible giants were not difficult? Yet who would say that their lives were not the par-adigm of meaning and fulfillment?

King David writes, "Had I not been preoccupied with Your Bible, I would have perished in my suffering."[2] Despite his life full of trials and tribulations, his psalms exude joy and grati-tude, because when one lives a meaningful life, pain and plea-sure coexist.[3] It's essential to understand that *pain does not make a person unhappy*—suffering does, and suffering is a consequence of our choices, not of our circumstances. Meaning fills our lives with pleasure and douses the flames of suffering. Struggles and setbacks are a part of life, but without perspective, they become our lives. Of course, we feel pain. It's part of the process—but we don't suffer unless we get stuck along the way.

I'VE GOT THE WHOLE WORLD IN MY HANDS

Humility does not spring from a sense of inferiority but bubbles forth from the fountain of reality. It's too easy to make the mistake of believing that humility is weakness; rather, it is strength. An arrogant person only takes from others. He has no capacity to give and so is not free. He is an emotional junkie, depending on others to feed his fragile ego—he's a slave to his own impulses, which he cannot rise above. When a person has humility, he is free because he is full—filled with gratitude; and gratitude and joy are intimately linked. If we think about the people we know who have a sense of gratitude, these same individuals are the most joyful. By contrast, those who lack appreciation for what they have live in a cycle of unrealized expectations and perpetual disappointment. They are filled with anger and resentment not because of anything major, but because their entire focus is on trivial matters that consume them with negativity. Let's connect the dots:

> The more responsible your choices (soul-oriented) →
> your self-esteem increases → your ego shrinks →
> your perspective widens → you perceive a greater
> context → your life (and life's challenges) has more
> meaning → [which results in pleasure] your humility
> stirs → your gratitude surges → and your joy flows.

> The less responsible your choices → your self-esteem
> decreases → your ego expands → your perspective
> narrows → you perceive a diminished context →
> your life (and life's challenges) loses meaning [you
> feel numb, depressed] → your arrogance grows →
> and this fuels frustration, anger, and resentment.

A healthy perspective fosters an organic attitude of gratitude, which itself changes the quality of our lives. (A summary of research findings on the benefits of gratitude is discussed in Chapter 28.) The only thing we truly have domain over is the quality of our choices, how we choose to live our lives. The wider and deeper our perspective in life, the more permanent and deep our gratitude. Nothing needs to happen to make us feel good. We simply appreciate what we have. When we are egocentric, we become angry and frustrated with life for disappointing us. Our expectations are never met, and we're consumed with thoughts of what we lack and what is owed to us. Happiness eludes us. We're always one step away from feeling complete, and we'll search endlessly for that next great thing that promises to bring us lasting fulfillment. Life becomes insufferable because as much good fortune as we receive, we are never fulfilled, because our focus is on what's missing and what's not good.

The egocentric psyche is not even deterred from pursuing an irrational or useless gain. So insidious is its desire for more, that even when we're racking up a high score on a video game, where our goal is the mere accrual of points, the brain's expectation mechanism is just as active. The ego doesn't care how useful something is—where there is something to be had, it wants it.[4]

Research shows that circumstances don't relate to life satisfaction, but subjective feelings do—and subjective feelings directly reflect our choices, not our conditions. The results of a study conducted at Harvard University bear this out. "Once we realize how much our reality depends on how we view it, it comes as less of a surprise that our external circumstances predict only about 10 percent of our total happiness."[5]

If we look around, we will notice that there are certain people who, no matter how fortunate their circumstances, are angry and unhappy, while there are those who endure unimaginable ordeals and move through life with an unshakable, deep sense of appreciation and joy. More important than the road we travel is who we become along the way. The ego too easily tricks us into accepting that what happens to us is the yardstick of significance. Yet it isn't the challenges we face, but how we face our challenges, that determines the true nature of the experience, and this is something we always have complete control over.

PART III
MAKING SENSE OF PAIN AND SUFFERING

9
Here Comes the Pain

Parts I and II of this book explored the psychological equation: The quality of our choices = the quality of our lives. In this section, we'll channel our psychological understanding into a larger spiritual context, to gain a deeper understanding of emotional health, in general, and of anger, in particular. As Abraham Maslow reminds us, "The spiritual life is part of the human essence. It is a defining characteristic of human nature . . ."

When a person experiences physical pain, he's unable to let his mind drift. He can't help but be absorbed in the present moment. Emotional pain has the same capacity to bring us into the present.[1] Pain, however, only acts as a fulcrum. It doesn't move us, but it gives us the opportunity to respond in one of three ways: (1) we can choose to avoid or dull the pain with endless distractions and excessive indulgence; (2) we can fortify our false self and become indignant, to compensate for feelings of weakness and vulnerability; or (3) we can act responsibly, accept the outcome, and seek meaning in the experience. If we see and accept a difficult reality— and get the message—then the pain pierces our shell, the ego. Instead of merely denting our image, the experience penetrates straight through to our soul. And we grow. Eminent psycholgist and

Holocaust survivor Frankl writes, "When we are no longer able to change a situation, we are challenged to change ourselves."[2]

We feel pain and label it "bad," but something that causes us emotional pain is not necessarily a bad thing. Is a person lying in a vegetative state, oblivious to pain, better off than one who endures life's daily struggles? Pain does not obstruct our growth. Pain functions as a necessary catalyst for growth, and growth is not negotiable—it is why we exist in the world, and without its prodding, we would never budge. Concerning the benefits of physical pain—how dangerous would life be if we didn't have pain receptors? If we accidentally leaned against a hot stove and didn't feel the heat, our flesh would burn. After falling, we might limp around with broken bones and cause ourselves more damage. Could we say that a person is better off not feeling the pain?

THE REAL YOU

To gain a greater understanding for life's difficulties, we need to pull back the lens further and look at *this life* within the larger context of our soul. Or, to put it more accurately, within the larger context of the real us. Because the truth is we do not have a soul. We *are* a soul, and we *have* a body.[3]

As we learned, challenges, in and of themselves, do not impinge on our happiness, nor do they cause us to become an angry person—but suffering does. Suffering is, as we discussed, the emotional consequence of ignoring reality and the opportunity for growth. Therefore, even if one doesn't embrace the soul's need to perfect itself, from a mental health standpoint the surest, swiftest, only real path to a satisfying, fulfilling, and pleasurable life is to greet reality with open arms. As we noted in Chapter 1, the research is definitive: Our tendency to avoid the pain inherent in taking responsibility for our lives is at the root of anger, and is central to nearly every emotional ailment. (We say *pain* rather than *challenge* because we don't shy away from encounters—even challenging ones—that we want to take on. Indeed, we may seek them out enthusiastically; and, too, we may run from tasks that are boring or arduous, but not because they are inherently difficult, but painful in that we find them uninteresting or uninspiring).

Let's remind ourselves that the more responsible our choices, the greater our self-esteem; the ego shrinks, and our perspective widens. We then gain context and meaning, which in turn give us pleasure (and reduce suffering), as well as the ability to feel empathy for others—to connect, to give love, and to receive love. Yet even with intense emotional pain, we still have the choice: We can suppress the pain and distract ourselves, feel angry and arrogant about our situation, or try to see the meaning in the experience and use it as an opportunity to grow. Should we resist reality, our struggle will be in vain. If we fail to act responsibly, all pain swells into suffering, and all suffering gives birth to anger. We sink lower and destroy ourselves from the inside out until we allow the self-correcting mechanism of pain to penetrate our shell and steer us in a healthier, more responsible direction. Some people respond when they see the light, others when they feel the heat, and still others will not budge until they get burned—and at times, not even then. What kind of person do you want to be? The answer to that question will determine the kind of life that you are going to lead.

WHY IS THIS MY CHALLENGE, ANYWAY?

Sometimes life just seems unfair. Outright painful. Downright difficult. Unjust. Yes, we control the quality of our lives and our emotional response to any given situation, but a major source of anger derives from the belief that we have received undeserved and excessive hardships. When, objectively speaking, we experience a double or triple helping of struggles that others are spared, this understandably challenges our sense of fairness. Even if we accept that certain ordeals inspire self-reflection and growth, why is a particular flaw inherent in us—the *soul*—in the first place?

In the following chapter, we'll explain this, as well as the force that protects the soul's mission, which helps us advance along the path we must travel and helps explain not only why seemingly bad things happen to good people, but the perhaps more nagging question, often paired with the first: *Why do good things happen to bad people?*

10
Why Good Things Happen to Bad People

Each of us has a unique purpose in this world, and our talents and strengths—and many of life's challenges—are tailor-made to help us accomplish what the soul requires. The word that most precisely describes this synced system is the Hebrew *mazal*. *Mazal*, literally "constellations," means the astrological influence that a person is born under (and refers to an inscrutable correlation between the natural world and a person's nature, having little to do with modern-day astrology, fortune-telling, and horoscopes.)

The word *mazal* is often translated as "luck," because, from our perspective, what happens to a person frequently appears to be random. What we fail to recognize is that for a person to complete his task in this world, he may, for example, enjoy undeserved riches or be faced with abject poverty. Therefore, one individual may do all the right things, yet still not seem to "catch a break," while another person effortlessly achieves success at every turn, sometimes despite himself. *Mazal* is more accurately defined as the confluence of conditions and circumstances that we require to complete, to perfect, ourselves. Before a person is born into this world, the instruments—the qualities and characteristics, the physical and mental abilities, and the means at his disposal—are synchronized to optimize the soul's path toward perfection.

Mazal is influential but not irrevocable or inescapable. We cannot expect that fate will swerve to intercept us, and that regardless of our efforts, good fortune or crisis will simply materialize to reveal an unalterable destiny. While *mazal* exists to expedite needed growth for the soul, we have to do our part, and we certainly cannot be negligent. Imagine, for instance, a person whose *mazal* dictates great wealth, but who chooses to spend his time with trivial pursuits. As fate would have it, he inherits one million dollars, which he promptly gambles at the racetrack. His *mazal* holds firm, and he wins. However, then he bets it all again and again and again. At some point, his *mazal* will run out. Our *mazal* helps us advance the path that we must travel and is synchronized to our life's purpose. Therefore, a person who forsakes accountability may lose whatever positive protection their *mazal* afforded him.

Due to the hidden influences of our soul, we're unable to gauge what is in the overall best interest of each *soul* and its purpose in this world. We can never say that a person injured or killed by a seemingly random event has abdicated his role or responsibility, for many great people have met with tragic, untimely deaths. A shared fate does not mean a shared spiritual level. We must never presume otherwise. Likewise, because we are each on our own level, a choice for one person is not necessarily a choice for another. Hence, the familiar dictum not to judge another person until you walk a mile in his shoes.

Naturally, people have different leanings and inborn desires which, Edmund Burke elegantly wrote, is not explained by reason, but rather "captivate the soul before the understanding is ready either to join with them, or to oppose them." We come into the world with a unique set of traits, none of which are inherently good or bad, but which can be channeled to be either constructive or destructive. Even the basest traits can be used for good. The preeminent psychologist Carl Jung explains, "Creative powers can just as easily turn out to be destructive. It rests solely with the moral personality whether they apply themselves to good things or to bad; and if this is lacking, no teacher can supply it or take its place."[1] Maslow, who established self-actualization as the pinnacle of human need, sums up the principle:

> A musician must make music, an artist must paint, a poet must write if he is to be at peace with himself. What a man can be, he must be. This is the need we may call self-actualization . . . it refers to man's desire for fulfillment, namely to the tendency for him to become actually in what he is potentially: to become everything that he is capable of becoming.[2]

Therefore, he should find a positive outlet for his inborn drives. He must direct any and all tendencies toward his growth, and if he fails to capitalize on their positive use, he will ultimately surrender to his unbridled desires and be governed by them.

Just as each person has a unique purpose with tailormade strengths, our weaknesses too are fashioned to maximize our potential; as Sigmund Freud writes, "Out of your vulnerabilities will come your strengths." Which means that a struggle for some people may not be for others. The challenges we face are sometimes universal and generic—for example, overcoming anger and laziness—and at other times unique to us, such as dealing with a specific physical limitation or emotional sensitivity. These factors set the tone for our experiences in life, but as we will recall, they remain irrelevant to one's satisfaction in life. Let's now remind ourselves what is explained in Chapter 8, because it's too easy to be fooled into thinking otherwise.

A VICTORY IN APPEARANCES ONLY

Should a person abdicate all personal responsibility, he may be successful in specific areas, but such prosperity is a hollow victory. It is indisputable that a person who lives irresponsibly moves away from his purpose and potential and will *de facto* suffer from a range of mental health issues that will hinder his enjoyment for what he has achieved or received. A blessing of long life to the depressed person becomes a self-imposed curse. The same is true for riches one uses to indulge in self-destructive vices. And although having a family is a blessing, it quickly becomes the opposite if we spend all of our time arguing with, or are estranged from, family members. In that case, it only wears on our emotional, spiritual, and physical health. Without perspective, our coping mechanism is disabled, and we simply feel as if the universe has heaped trouble after trouble upon us. All of the good in our life remains out of focus and we are left in a state of restless desire, goaded on by a sense of entitlement, with a predictable finale: disappointment and despair.

Regardless of what life serves us, we can make the bitter pill more palatable and perhaps, if we choose to be extraordinary, turn it into a lavish feast. The soul's mission and corresponding *mazal* affects happenstance, but as we learned, our happiness and emotional health are a function of choice. Life's challenges are not equally distributed to everyone, but the power of choice is the great equalizer.

11
Staying Sane in an Insane World

When we know a matter is insignificant, we obviously keep our emotional investment to a minimum. Although a person with perspective sees the irrelevance of an event that might overwhelm his egocentric counterpart, the question everyone faces is, "How do we manage what *is* relevant?" To answer this, we'll turn to the subject of trust, and explore more deeply how the quality of our choices gives us access to a deep level of calm.

ENTER GOD
Difficult times and tragic events challenge our coping skills. As humans, our perspective is finite, which makes it difficult for us to see the bigger picture. Still, we can gain peace of mind and derive comfort during trying times when we develop the capacity to trust, which then serves as a surrogate to our sight. In that way, we become immune to distress because we don't have to see something with our own two eyes in order to accept that the outcome is for our ultimate benefit.

We can have *faith* that things will work out for the best, but we may still be plagued by worry and moments of doubt. When we have *trust*, however, negative thoughts don't fill our mind. We don't dwell on, or become consumed with, the outcome. Trust is an intellectual process, a natural outgrowth of our positive choices, and it exists independently of our mood or emotional state. The difference is profound. If you have faith that a rickety bridge will hold you, you might walk across it, but with some trepidation. Trust, in contrast, is unequivocal and unwavering and means that you choose to walk across the bridge without hesitation, with much less anxiety or fear. This is important to understand because as we know, fear breeds anger, so if we turn off the faucet of fear, then we shut down the flow of anger.

How do we move from faith to trust? No leap of faith is required. The decision to exercise self-control eliminates anger and anxiety because it moves us beyond faith in God and into trust in God. Here's how it works: We can't trust in God beyond the scope of our behavior. When we make a poor choice—meaning that we refuse to accept reality and respond properly—we are not acknowledging God, and to the degree that He is not in our lives, we can't have a relationship with Him, let alone trust in Him. The chasm widens afterward when we justify our actions; this behavior further torques the ego and pushes God still further away. We feel this distance as a lack of faith. Yet we don't lose faith in God without first losing faith in ourselves. It is we who have changed. When we turn away from what is right, all of our relationships inevitably suffer—including our relationship with God.

Someone who is in the habit of ignoring reality cannot simply bring God into his life, conjure Him up, and trust in Him at the moment of his choosing to soothe an anxious thought or calm a troubled mind, because the ego is precisely what blocks trust in God. Trust is a natural by-product of humility, not of arrogance.

Fear breeds in the waters of disconnectedness, between our awareness of the truth and our behavior, and the greater the disparity, the greater the fear.

Productive living is the heartiest expression of our trust in the future, in God, and in ourselves. A person who feels too afraid (of the pain) to make long-range plans and to invest in his life sends a message to his subconscious that he does not have *trust*. Then, imperceptibly and unintentionally, he seeks to validate his fears and becomes attuned to whatever in his world offers him proof that he is right. Because of his ego-based decision to avoid legitimate pain—and opt out of life—his ego must now prove him right.

In short, action converts faith into trust. We can't establish trust in God if we don't live our lives in a way that demonstrates our belief in God. Abraham's ten trials nourished his relationship with God, each adding a strand of trust in a bond that culminated in total submission to His will, without question or compunction. With the first test, God sought to assure Abraham, "I will make of you a great nation; I will bless you, and make your name great and you shall be a blessing."[1] By the last test, such reassurance had become unnecessary, even though the command itself was exceedingly more difficult and seemingly contradicted God's initial assertion.[2] Such is the bond of trust.

SELF-CONTROL = PEACE OF MIND

We intuit—via our conscience, the soul—that with each of our acts, a natural consequence occurs. When we engage in conduct that we know to be wrong, no matter how masterfully we justify it, the voice of our soul cries out in shame. Although the ego often muffles the soul's cry, we unconsciously wait for the universe to drop the other proverbial shoe.

Imagine the following scenario: A thief walks into a grocery store, steals a loaf of bread, and then flees, probably looking over his shoulder nervously for the negative consequences of his action. For a while after the adventure, he will be tormented by what might happen. Just as a person braces himself physically in anticipation of being hit, so, too, do we brace ourselves emotionally when we feel vulnerable. If the thief had not stolen the bread, such anxiety would not exist.

Individuals with high life-change scores (that is, they experience multiple life changes at one time) are more likely to fall ill. Yet most surprisingly, studies reveal that the illness correlates with *any type of change*.[3] Whether we perceive the event as positive or negative has no effect on the stress we experience; rather, the stress level is determined by our need to control what is happening. This is why we may find ourselves engaging in self-destructive behavior, even when things in our lives go particularly well.

The path to living anger free is paved not by circumstances, but by choice. An individual who controls himself recognizes that he doesn't control the world, and so he is not anxious. In fact, this understanding offers solace because all he has to do is exercise self-control, and God will take care of the rest. Conversely, one who cannot control himself falsely believes—courtesy of his ego—that he is, or should be, in control, and so becomes anxious in uncertain times and angry when reality unfolds against his expectations. His foolish quest to control that which is beyond his control will only lead him to lose more control over himself. This is a nuanced, yet critical, point. The more self-control we have, the more we see—and accept—what is within our control and what is not. Therefore we can, as the saying goes, *let go and let God*, because we know that when we have done all we can, God will do all we can't.

Whatever the character trait, if we don't possess it, we can't see it in others or feel it in ourselves. A person who doesn't love himself can't fully love others or feel their love, and a person who doesn't trust himself distrusts others and is often not trusted by others. Those who lack self-control have no concept of trust. How can they trust in God when, in their world, "trust" is a theoretical concept and not part of their inner reality? God is infinite and unchanging. If we want to see His hand in our lives, if we want to trust in Him, it is we who must change. We must make different choices. There is no alternate truth.

TRUST = ACCEPTANCE = ANGER FREE

Acceptance means we do not ignore reality, and if the reality is that we are in pain, then the height of responsibility is to recognize that this is a moment to be in pain. It's perfectly healthy, even obligatory, to feel this way. If we process the experience with patience and compassion for ourselves, then we move more swiftly to acceptance. If, however, the ego is active, then we become filled with self-pity or false shame, we delay acceptance and add an unnecessary layer of suffering. Self-pity judges our pain to be unfair—*poor me. I live an unfair life in an unjust world, suffering a cruel, undeserved fate.* False shame declares our pain is justified because we are unworthy of good and of happiness.

The upcoming process in Part IV is critical because it allows us to see and accept that a painful ordeal does not mean that God has rejected us or abandoned us because we are unworthy of His love. God's love for us does not diminish because we feel unworthy—but our capacity to feel His love for us, does. As we have learned, people who do not love themselves conclude that others don't either. They feel that people do unkind things to them intentionally, rarely assigning a benign motivation to such behavior. Their worldview is similarly skewed, which further distances them from God and shatters their self-esteem. They tell themselves, *If God is doing this to me, then I must be bad.* This idea perpetuates a negative self-image, spiraling them further away from their potential and any motivation to invest in themselves and in their future.

If we are angry at God because of our own faults and limitations, trials and tribulations, then we are not living in the world of truth; we will constantly take out our frustrations on ourselves and everyone around us. The famed philosopher Friedrich Nietzsche writes, "He who has a *why* to live for can bear almost any *how.*" Fundamentally, trust in God means the acceptance and recognition that all our experiences come to us directly from God, all out of His love for us. It means knowing in one's heart that there is no such thing as chance, and that all of our life experiences are under complete and total Divine supervision.

Unlike faith, trust directly reflects our relationship with God. The closer we are to Him, the stronger our trust, and the greater our recognition that everything He does is specifically for our good. The message is, "You matter to Me." The entire mechanism of self-esteem is geared toward creating ourselves into a vessel that is capable of recognizing and receiving God's love for us. Only then do we live with the perpetual awareness that He takes an intimate and personal interest in every aspect of our lives, and that everything we do matters deeply to Him. Absent self-esteem, we cannot help but feel that we do not matter to God, that we are irrelevant. Nothing is more painful or false.

PART IV

MAKE PEACE WITH THE PAST, FOR GOOD

12
Planes of Acceptance

We have discussed that to the extent we refuse to accept the truth about ourselves and our lives, we are forced to distort the world around us to align with our preferred, less-painful version of reality. Therefore, to accept reality, we must accept ourselves; and to fully accept ourselves, we need to make peace with our past and plan for our future. First things first.

SELF-ACCEPTANCE

The truth cannot be offended or upended by reality. Images need protection. The truth does not. If we fully accept ourselves, we have no need to project an image. We have nothing to protect and nothing to hide from. We become more real, through and through. Shakespeare lyrically rendered this creed in the following verse:

> *This above all: to thine own self be true,*
> *And it must follow, as the night the day,*
> *Thou canst not then be false to any man.*[1]

Jung stated that every part of the personality we don't love will become hostile to us. Becoming more courageous means that we must face ourselves, because it is self-discovery that we actually fear. This is self-evident. We are not easily offended when faced with a truth that we fully acknowledge, nor are we bothered by a blatant, bold-faced lie. Only when presented with a truth that we refuse to recognize do we become sensitive or self-conscious. Total self-acceptance ensures that we don't connect the dots to let another person's actions point to a deficiency within ourselves.

Have you ever noticed the following to be true? Once you've fully accepted a facet of yourself or of your life, you don't hide from it anymore. You don't care who knows, who finds out, and you certainly don't let it hold you back. Now imagine a life where there is total and complete acceptance. No masks. No games. No pretending. When you no longer hide from yourself, your false identity dissolves because its only purpose was to keep you from seeing yourself. At this point, your fears dissolve because there is no longer the threat of exposing your real self to yourself, or to others. You become free because you are shame free, and with this freedom, you become anger free.

ACCEPTANCE IS NOT APPROVAL

We often confuse acceptance and approval. This erroneous thinking not only negates the concept of unconditional love, but also impairs our ability to accept ourselves, faults and all. Acceptance doesn't mean that we sit back and resign ourselves to victimhood. To the contrary, acceptance is the path to growth. If I want to go from Point A to Point B, I first need to acknowledge that I'm at Point A. If I hide from myself—who I am and where I am—then I will never be able to move forward. Acceptance is not passivity, but the seed of change, because we cannot grow beyond that which we refuse to accept even exists. The paradoxical theory of change states that "Change occurs when one becomes what he is, not when he tries to become what he is not. . . . One must first fully experience what one is before recognizing all the alternatives of what he may be."[2]

Let's introduce another quote by Carl Jung: "Everything that irritates us about others can lead us to an understanding of ourselves." If we accept ourselves, we also avoid a powerful anger trigger—the mirror effect. It has often been said that we feel annoyed by traits in others that we ourselves possess. This isn't quite true. The very reason that we're able to perceive certain faults in others may be because they lie within ourselves, but observing the trait and becoming upset by it are two very different things. Our intellectual observation becomes emotionally charged only when we have not yet accepted this fault within ourselves. If we accept a failing in ourselves, seeing it emerge in another evokes great empathy, because we know just what this person is going through. We can see through the lens of love and kindness, and we can better help him become more self-aware.

When the person sees that our motivation is pure and out of love, it's an entirely different conversation than if our ego is involved, because then our words will feel like an attack rather than an act of kindness. Any rebuke that comes from a place of anger or resentment is not going to be offered or received as a loving observation. In Proverbs, King Solomon wrote, "Just as water reflects a face to a face, so does the heart of man reflect one to another."[3]

SEALING THE ENERGY LEAK

The quality of our lives hinges on the quality of our choices. True enough—but is this *enough?* Many of us walk around bruised and battered by—take your pick—trauma, tragedy, an abusive childhood, abusive relationships, or sick or evil people who have walked through our lives and walked over us. What can we do with that message playing over and over in our minds—a message that courses through our veins, saying, "I'm worthless"?

As was discussed in Chapter 8, perspective gives us the natural ability to frame a trauma in a meaningful context before it becomes fused with our identity and part of a self-sustaining story that defines us. Yet when the trauma occurs during our formative years, it's difficult to break free because the story is all controlling and all consuming—it's the only narrative we know. To move our lives forward we must face ourselves; and to love and accept what we see—we must face our past.

13
Trauma, Tragedy, and Triggers

When we feel powerless over the unknown, we may become angry to feed the illusion of control—even if that anger is directed at ourselves. Have you ever heard someone say, "The worst is not knowing?" Even bad—painful—news may be welcomed over the unknown. Similarly, *the world hurts me in ways that I cannot predict or control, but by harming myself I gain control over my own pain*. We will inflict pain upon ourselves—completely self-destruct, if we must—simply to be in control of it. In doing so, we have removed the greater threat: the debilitating, merciless pain of fear. We have made our pain predictable and known. Feelings of guilt ("I have hurt another; I did wrong") and shame ("I am bad; I am less") intensify our motivation for self-harm because we want to punish ourselves, to exact justice, to right the wrongs.

This deeply flawed approach to pain management takes an inevitably crueler turn, because the fear of uncontrolled pain is eclipsed by the pain of feeling nothing at all. When we attempt to bypass the pain of living we become numb to life itself and the real tragedy is not that we have lost our way, but that we do not care that there is a way.

THE POWER OF DECISION

Whatever the situation, whatever the horror—neglect, humiliation, abandonment—when we understand that anger is a choice,
we begin to seal the breach in our self-esteem. Many people might
have treated us poorly, even abusively, and no doubt bear fault for
our ensuing self-destructive behaviors. Yet right here and now,
blame won't move us forward in life. It won't make us one bit
happier or more fulfilled. Taking responsibility now, however,
will. This isn't a question of whether we delay deciding or do it
immediately. We are making a choice every moment of every day
to hold on to resentment or let it go.

The quality of our lives is directly proportional to the amount
of responsibility we willingly accept for what we can control. Living responsibly means that you maximize that control. In every
instant, you have a say in what happens. You make a choice. In
magical moments, you stop repeating the futile mantra of "How
did I get here?" or "I can't help myself," and instead open yourself up to a new possibility: "What is within my control right now
that will help me to value who I am? To remind myself that I am
a person of dignity and worthy of self-respect."

RETHREADING THE GIFT OF ACCEPTANCE

Total acceptance includes the acknowledgment that some of life's
most painful ordeals are beyond our understanding, much less our
comprehension. Once we come to this place of acceptance, the
ego will no longer force its own destructive narrative. The ego
demands to know *why*. If we accept or, better still, embrace, the
unknown—that although we cannot fathom *why,* we know that
the *why* is geared toward the soul's ultimate good—then we are
free. If we allow our ego to get the better of us, then it will take

over our worldview, highjacking our values and distorting our beliefs in a futile attempt to forge a *known* out of an *unknown*.

It is normal and natural—as well as healing and healthy—to mine our experiences for meaning, to try to gain insight and understanding. Yet, to whatever degree we fall short, we cannot fabricate a reason, because that reason is false, and this falsehood puts a stranglehold on the entirety of our lives. Then what passes for living one's life is really a response to trauma. Let's look at the psychology involved.

Statistically speaking, a woman who is highly promiscuous and engaged in rampant, casual sex or prostitution was most likely sexually abused, in some fashion, as a girl or young adult—more than 85 percent of prostitutes have been sexually abused in childhood. To reconcile and make sense of what happened to her, this woman is forced, albeit subconsciously, to reduce the significance of the event. By diluting the value and sanctity of sexual relations, her willful promiscuity makes what happened to her feel less painful. Simply put, the value of what was harmed, or taken from her, has been reduced. (Though futile, the ego also attempts to dilute associated feelings of vulnerability and helplessness by experiencing the re-expression of the trauma again and again, but with her in charge each time.)

Devaluing intimacy to the point of insignificance reinforces her attitude that it does not matter; or perhaps she will conclude the she doesn't matter, in which case it also makes sense. What's the harm in damaging someone who is worthless? If this is her conclusion then a host of self-destructive behaviors will quickly follow suit to reinforce that she is indeed nothing, and not worth investing in, caring for, or protecting. Certainly all is well and just in the world if a worthless person is abused. Where's the harm in that? Throwing garbage into a garbage can makes sense. Of course, courtesy of misplaced shame, she may conclude that she is to blame, in which case she did this to herself. The ego can live with that. (Parenthetically, this is not unlike the warped solace one may take upon learning that an accident victim contributed to his fate. He was drinking; he was an abusive person. This makes sense to us. He was not an innocent random casualty of an undeserved fate. He had it coming.) The soul recognizes absolute justice lies beyond the veil of the finite, but the ego insists on drawing connections and concocting conclusions to explain the unexplainable—and to remove a stain of shame that doesn't exist.

There is not always a *why* that we can understand from our limited perspective. Once we are willing to accept this, we no longer live in a personality created with the singular objective of making sense of that which is unknowable. We move toward freedom. We move toward life.

14

It's Not Too Late to Have a Happy Childhood

Even when we strive every which way—to be good and to do good—we can find a hole in our self-esteem thanks to childhood. Before we begin laying blame, it's important to recall that even a child whose parents do everything right (theoretically) will still transition to adulthood with imperfect self-esteem. A person's self-esteem may have been injured by academic issues, social factors, or health problems; but in and of themselves, none of these are more detrimental than growing up in a house with a parent who suffers from low self-esteem—and not necessarily because of overt abuse.

Children who are raised in a loving and nurturing environment can also suffer emotionally if a parent becomes unusually overprotective. This instills a climate of fear and dread into every aspect of life that is unknown or unpredictable, and causes children to be overly self-conscious and anxious—and fear, we know, is the precursor to anger. Such children typically develop into adults who are sensitive to rejection, emotionally fragile, and who lack confidence. While well-intentioned, overprotective behavior is indicative of the parent's own lack of self-esteem, with any one or more of the following motivations and manifestations: The parent a) cannot bear for his child to be afraid or hurt (a projection of his own fears and insecurities); b) is fearful that the child will not love him or will become angry with him if discipline is used; c) wants the child to be his friend and is uncomfortable exerting appropriate and responsible authority; and/or d) desires that the child be forever dependent on the parent so he can fill his own emotional holes by feeling useful and/or maintaining control over the child's life.[1]

The above notwithstanding, a pronounced impact to an adult's self-esteem is often owed to his suffering from lack of properly expressed love or experiencing intense turmoil at an early age. For egocentric beings (children), it is easy to ascribe a failure within themselves as the reason behind a parent's behavior. What seven-year-old child is going to say to himself, *Wow, Dad just lost that big account at work, so he's letting off a little steam and taking it out on me. But that's okay; I know it's got nothing to do with me. He's just having a hard day.* A parent becomes angry with the child, and so the child naturally concludes that there is a flaw within himself. Enter, shame. He translates his parent's anger into, "I am unworthy of his love," which soon becomes, "I am not worthy of being loved." Now, if a child can form these conclusions—as many do—with loving parents, imagine how easy it is for the child to draw the conclusion that he is unlovable or bad when he is being raised by abusive parents.

If we did not receive love from our parents as children, or felt that our lives were out of control due to trauma or domestic volatility, we may needlessly spend the rest of our lives thirsting for love and acceptance. Everything we do is intended to bring us to that end; but there is no end because you cannot fix what is not broken. We are already whole. We have always been whole.

The love that parents give children is determined by their own limitations, not those of the children. It never occurs to us as children that maybe it has nothing to do with us. If a mother is capable of love, she will be loving to all of her children, even one who turns out to be a murderer. But if she lacks the ability to love, then even an innocent well-mannered child will be subject to her hostility, because she is incapable of giving. As adults, we can still find it difficult to appreciate that our self-worth is not contingent on our parents' acceptance of us. Recall that the ego concocted the equation: *How someone treats me is a reflection of my self-worth.* This is not so. We are not less because someone can't love us.

If we saw a person in a wheelchair, we wouldn't get mad at him because he can't get up and walk. Somebody who is emotionally handicapped is equally challenged. Does it make sense to resent a parent for not being able to give us something that he or she doesn't have? Do we want to hold on to anger because our mother or father was, and still may be, incapable of loving us? People give love. If they don't have it, then they can't give it, regardless of how desperately their soul yearns to love their own child. As we discussed in Chapter 4, how someone treats us—even if it's our parents—provides a window into their own feelings of self-worth or lack thereof, but it reveals nothing of our self-worth. The question we want to ask ourselves is, *"What kind of person would I be today, if I were treated differently as a child?"* Whoever that person is, *is* who you really are.

DOUBLE WHAMMY

Relationship issues with our parents often affect our relationship with God for two interlacing reasons. One, a poor—let's call it complicated—relationship with a parent (or parents) often injures the child's self-esteem, in which case he will have difficulty feeling and accepting God's love for him; inevitably, the choices he makes will further entangle the ego and continue to squeeze God out of his life. Second, a parent is the first authority figure in a child's life, so a child who was mistreated by a parent (or by anyone in authority) may have difficulty accepting, let alone trusting, the ultimate authority of God.

The Ten Commandments are divided into two categories: The first five contain the man-to-God commandments, and the second five, the man-to-man commandments. Revealingly, the fifth commandment to honor our parents is on the man-to-God side of the tablets. This is because we don't find it easy to love, and to feel loved by, the Creator of the universe while holding on to anger toward our parents. On many levels, the relationship between child and parent symbolizes and, often determines, our relationship with God. By honoring our parents (or at least not hating, and acknowledging that they have their own "baggage" and are suffering themselves) we cultivate an appreciation for, and an understanding of, how much our parents love us (or perhaps long to), despite their limitations. This awareness then enhances our relationship with God because it helps us to recognize that there are no limitations to God's total and unconditional love for us.

An emotionally healthy person will not have considerable unresolved anger toward a parent. It is highly improbable that anyone can enjoy positive, let alone deep and meaningful, relationships while this anger exists. Anyone who feels anger toward a parent must make it a priority to move past it—or, better, to reframe the negative feelings into more accurate and positive feelings.

REFRAMING THE PAST

A shift in perspective now allows us to undo our perception of the past by reframing it—and permanently alter how we see ourselves and our world. Recall that context gives rise to meaning, so by reframing the past and putting it into a different context, we change what it means—instantly and automatically. Let's take a banal example from everyday life. How often does a book's ending make or break the book? Do we find it less enjoyable because of a silly ending? Sort of. We read it and enjoy it, but the ending changes the enjoyment of what we have just read. And, too, an exciting twist at the end shines a new light on the entire story— we replay in our minds the scenes we thought meant one thing, but ahh, now we see something else entirely. Everything changes.

It's difficult for us to grasp the concept that reality is not linear and that a shift in perspective can create retroactive changes in our attitude, feelings, and thoughts. But let's imagine an elderly woman who, after believing that she was happily married for sixty years, is told on her deathbed that her recently departed husband never loved her—that her parents had paid him $10 million to marry her, and, on top of that, he had a secret life with another wife in a different city. Can we say that she was happy her entire life and that only her last thirty seconds were difficult? Did the birthday celebrations, anniversaries, walks, conversations, laughter, and memories of beautiful vacations disappear? No. They are there in her memory, but they've changed. Her past is now different. If, after she heard this revelation, someone were to ask this woman, "How was your life?" what would she answer? Would she easily say, "Wonderful"? More likely, she would say, "Awful, sad, and heartbreaking." The characters and the events are still fixed in time, but we can glimpse how the "now" has an impact on what came before it.

That's not to say we should try to convince ourselves that our past carries no meaning. Instead, we should simply allow for the possibility that the meaning we assigned to events might not be true, and that how we feel about ourselves based on a damaged relationship or trauma is an inaccurately formed conclusion. We don't have to hate ourselves because someone else hates us. We don't have to harm ourselves because some else harmed us. We are not unlovable because someone is incapable of loving us.

A RETURN ON OUR INVESTMENT

Research shows that forgiveness not only restores positive feelings toward the offender, but also, "may spill over beyond the relationship with the offender, promoting generalized prosocial orientation."[2] In other words, when we forgive someone who has hurt us, all of our relationships seem to benefit. The opposite is also true. Unresolved anger from a soured relationship will seep into our other relationships.

This is a function of human design, whereby we hold on to painful experiences (physical, as well as psychological), in order to learn from those experiences and to avoid repeating them. Until we acknowledge them, they remain part of us. Think of the events in your life that you refuse to release, and contrast them with those you have accepted. The brain develops specific pathways to alert you to a potential threat, and the wiring remains in effect until you process out the emotion.[3] The more we ruminate and re-energize the wrongs, the stronger the neural pathways become, and we wire ourselves to become angry and resentful people—to everyone. When we hold on to anger, we are the ones who suffer—emotionally, spiritually, and physically. Biofeedback shows an instant increase in stress when a person has anger-producing thoughts or recalls memories of insult or resentment. Correspondingly, feelings of forgiveness instantly lower stress levels, producing a host of chemical and neuromuscular changes in the person.

The physical and emotional benefits of forgiveness are well documented. Forgiveness is directly correlated to a person experiencing less anxiety, stress, and hostility, as well as fewer symptoms of depression, and less risk of alcohol and substance abuse.[4] Other research finds forgiveness to be positively associated with five measures of health: physical symptoms, medications used, sleep quality, fatigue, and somatic conditions.[5]

GIVING AND LOVING

When a person gives, he loves the person he gives to even more—and so he plants love, and it grows. A child primarily receives and a parent typically gives—which person usually loves the other more? Some children can't wait to get out of the house, while the parent remains forever concerned with the child's well-being. Every positive emotion stems from giving and flows outward from us to others, whereas every negative emotion revolves around our taking from others.

Studies prove that we are inclined to dislike others more after we do them harm because we are unconsciously driven to distance ourselves emotionally in an attempt to reduce the *cognitive dissonance*. The internal conflict we create is, *Why did I do this to this person?* The justification must then become, *It must be because I really don't like him and/or he deserves it!* Otherwise, we are forced to consider the possibility that perhaps we are not such good people or act unfairly and unjustly. This principle works in reverse, too. We like people more after doing something nice for them. If we do someone a favor, for example, we're likely to have positive feelings toward that person. An excerpt from Benjamin Franklin's autobiography:

My first promotion was my being chosen, in 1736, clerk of the General Assembly. The choice was made that year without opposition; but the year following, when I was again propos'd (the choice, like that of the members, being annual), a new member made a long speech against me, in order to favour some other candidate. I was, however, chosen, which was the more agreeable to me, as, besides the pay for the immediate service as clerk, the place gave me a better opportunity of keeping up an interest among the members, which secur'd to me the business of printing the votes, laws, paper money, and other occasional jobs for the public, that, on the whole, were very profitable.

I therefore did not like the opposition of this new member, who was a gentleman of fortune and education, with talents that were likely to give him, in time, great influence in the House, which, indeed, afterwards happened. I did not, however, aim at gaining his favour by paying any servile respect to him, but, after some time, took this other method. Having heard that he had in his library a certain very scarce and curious book, I wrote a note to him, expressing my desire of perusing that book, and requesting he would do me the favour of lending it to me for a few days. He sent it immediately, and I return'd it in about a week with another note, expressing strongly my sense of the favour. When we next met in the House, he spoke to me (which he had never done before), and with great civility; and he ever after manifested a readiness to serve me on all occasions, so that we became great friends, and our friendship continued to his death. This is another instance of the truth of an old maxim I had learned, which says, *"He that has once done you a kindness will be more ready to do you another, than he whom you yourself have obliged."* And it shows how much more profitable it is prudently to . . . return, and continue inimical proceedings.[6]

In Chapter 23, we explore a fascinating phenomenon called *facial feedback hypothesis*, which states that an incongruous expression or behavior forces the subconscious to recalibrate our feelings and beliefs, in order to reconcile itself. Not only is this effective in the moment, but it also helps mitigate our hostility or disdain toward another person. This is particularly effective to use with people closest to us, whom we might behave passive-aggressively toward. It's a powerful way to uproot our latent anger.

Regardless of the relationship status, even if we want nothing to do with this person, we will still find it highly useful to forgive, because forgiveness allows us to let go of the past and ease our lives forward. Even if the person is no longer alive, we can best melt away our resentment by doing something in this person's memory—give to a charity, perform an act of kindness, plant a tree, bring flowers to the grave. We need to do something, anything, to reinforce our desire to let go and to move on.

There comes a time when we have to ask ourselves, *How much time and effort does it take for me to stoke the flames of anger, and how much more of my life will I devote to doing this?* Even in the case of serious and significant wrongdoing, forgiveness doesn't mean that we deny the hurt, forget that it happened, or recuse the offender of responsibility or accountability; it means that we're not going to allow this person to destroy our potential, to harm us anymore. At its core, forgiveness is a choice to give up our role as a victim.

15
My Apologies, Please

Most of our anger issues stem from our unwillingness to deal—aka *face the pain*—with either something someone did to us (producing anger), or something we did (producing guilt or shame—which is anger turned inward). Unless we act responsibly now, to "right our wrongs," we will find a steady leak in our self-esteem.

FORGIVENESS BEGINS AT HOME
Have you ever noticed that when you're angry with yourself, you're more prone to bang into things or knock them over? Through such behavior, we unconsciously attempt to get back at ourselves for making a decision that we have remorse over. Guilt, a negative force, weighs us down, causing us to engage in unconsciously motivated self-harm. According to research—and common sense—guilt gives rise to self-destructive tendencies and makes us desire to suffer or be punished.[1]

We must be able to forgive ourselves for the damage we've done to others *and* to ourselves. Taking responsibility is not about being perfect—it's what we do when we discover that we have faltered, and how we move forward to make things right after we have done wrong. The ability to forgive ourselves, rather than self-flagellate, increases our accountability—which then leads to regaining our self-control and initiating a course correction.[2] Using an MRI, scientists demonstrated the neurobiological basis for why self-compassion helps us self-regulate. When we show warmth and compassion to ourselves, we elicit *neuroaffective* responses similar to those stimulated by an encouraging, supportive other.[3] This then helps us feel loved and supported, making us aware that we deserve better, and it instills in us the will to invest in our long-term care and benefit.[4] In addition, the more forgiving you are of your own setbacks—when you let yourself down—the easier it will be for you to forgive others when you feel they let you down.

Guilt ("I have hurt another; I did wrong") and shame ("I am bad; I am less *because* of what I did") are useless unless they create the impetus for action, in which case what we really feel is regret. We can't "talk away" or rationalize our behavior, but we can transform our negative feelings into positive emotions by turning guilt or shame into regret and regret into action.

First, we must resolve in our hearts never to commit the same act again. If it was a one-time action, then there is nothing more to stop. However, if we still keep engaging in the behavior that we feel bad about, then we must stop it. If we can't refrain immediately, we must create a plan to stop this behavior over a period of time, and we must stick to the plan. We need to create deterrents for ourselves, to avoid repeating the same transgression. In this way, we make a firm declaration to ourselves and others that we have really changed, and we're doing what we can to ensure that our new-and-improved self thrives. Finally, we have to *right our wrongs* as best we can (see subchapter below).

The ego favors suffering that is known, so we retreat to the relative sanctuary of self-inflicted wounds. But the genesis of growth—the key to getting unstuck—begins the moment we look at ourselves, not with condemnation, blame, and judgment, but with love, compassion, and patience. We will come to discover that we are not bad. We are in pain from what has been done to us, and by us. We are hurt and we have caused hurt.

A person who holds on to guilt or shame is not being noble, he is being selfish. Indulging his despair is the height of irresponsibility, well beyond whatever act led to feelings of guilt in the first place. He wraps himself in the comfortable numbness of self-pity—the drug that's always within reach and never runs out—to avoid facing the pain of himself, his actions, and his life. He declares that he is worthless—so damaged, bad, and broken that he is beyond repair or reproach. This unconsciously motivated, ego-driven tactic cleverly recuses him of responsibility because he doesn't deserve to be happy. He thereby avoids the pain of accountability and the burden of obligation.

SETTING THINGS STRAIGHT

Forgiving and apologizing both give us a taste of emotional freedom. This is why we typically feel good afterward. We give an apology, and we give forgiveness. Only when we are free can we give, and this single act promotes our independence and builds our emotional immunity. Yet before we attempt to gain forgiveness for ourselves, we must move forward with the utmost delicacy. When we've clearly violated the respect, trust, and rights of another, the path to forgiveness lies in *restoring balance* to the relationship—be it personal or professional. In balance, we find justice, and in justice, we find forgiveness. Follow this six-phase protocol as best you can to do your part in bringing peace to your relationships and yourself.

Phase 1: Humility and Respect

If we enter the situation with anything other than *complete humility,* we likely won't receive forgiveness. We must negate our ego. *It's not about us,* it's about the other person. This means we should not argue and scream our point or show up at someone's office demanding that he listen to our side of the story. Rather, we should ask permission before we speak to him and perhaps even *prior* to initiating personal contact—via a note or intermediary— if the relationship is severely strained. Approaching the person with extreme deference and even reverence is a requisite for the process. We want to ask for permission before we do anything. We should leave right away if he doesn't want to talk to us. We can try again another time. (And if we're there only to be yelled at, that's fine, too.) In our anger, we often do the opposite of this, and say such things as, "I drove all the way here, so you darn well better talk to me. I said I was sorry! What more do you want?" This adds fuel to the flames as we further demonstrate lack of respect. We *almost* don't have to say anything, as long as the other person sees that we're doing everything possible to make things right again.

In a situation where the person won't even talk to us or we haven't been in contact for some time, we might need to jump-start the relationship and put in a great deal of effort, such as flying to where the person is, dropping off a letter of apology, and then leaving without speaking to the person. If we can make an investment—emotionally, financially, or any other way—and show genuine effort, even without immediate success, we will gain traction.

Phase 2: Be Accountable

It's important for us to take full and complete responsibility for our actions. We must not shift the blame or make excuses—this will only exacerbate the situation. We shouldn't say, "I got so upset because we did . . . ," or, "I didn't think it was a big deal to . . ." We must not blame the person for anything—his actions or ours—and we mustn't minimize our role.

Phase 3: Sincerely Apologize

Sometimes we forget to actually say the words *I'm sorry.* Though these words are rarely enough, they are necessary to gaining forgiveness. Moreover, we must acknowledge that our actions hurt the other person: *I'm sorry, I know I hurt you and caused you pain.* We need to ensure that our sincerity comes across. An insincere apology won't be believed; and if we're not believed, we won't be forgiven. If we aren't truly sorry and remorseful, then we may repeat our behavior and put this person through more pain—in which case it might be time for us to reevaluate the relationship and ourselves.

Phase 4: Be Willing to Accept – and Even Offer – Consequences

It's one thing to talk the talk, but things can fall apart if he thinks that we're trying to escape unscathed. Let the other person know that you're willing to face and accept all consequences of your actions. Putting ourselves in the hands of someone we have harmed and being answerable for our conduct and the aftermath will help to mitigate that person's feelings of vulnerability and insecurity. Our initial act, which requires forgiveness, pulled the emotional rug right out from under him. Our behavior violated trust, which is the cornerstone of a relationship. By putting this person in charge of your fate and the entirety of the relationship, you help to reestablish a sense of security and give back, in a way, the power that you took.

We can start by saying something like, "I know what I did was wrong. You have every right to be angry with me. I'm willing to accept the full repercussions of my actions." We must begin to cede control with our words, or he may further castigate us as his way of setting things straight.

Phase 5: Make Things Right

If we profited in some way, then we must give back what doesn't rightfully belong to us, in order to set things straight—whether it be money or other items. If we don't have what we wrongfully took but we can replace it, we must make every effort to do so as soon as possible—and when feasible, we have to let the person know our plan and our progress. *And remember: It's essential to continue on this path even if he still isn't talking to us.*

Regardless of our relationship with the person, by doing what is right, despite not getting what we want (the relationship), we can prove that we are the kind of person he wants back in his life. It is important to stress here that whether or not there is something tangible to return, we are obligated to work on the character flaw or emotional issue that led to our hurtful actions. Only in this way can we authentically declare what we are now—or are working hard toward becoming: a different person who is no longer capable of such abhorrent conduct.

Phase 6: A Painless Game Plan

Let the person know that he has full power over how things proceed, that he is in control every step of the way. You *suggest* a game plan that moves slowly but surely toward reestablishing the relationship while ensuring that at any time, he can opt to continue, stop, or change course.

NOT SUCCESSFUL, NO PROBLEM

Have you ever driven by a bad traffic accident and noticed that the passengers in your car suddenly become *nicer* to one another? There's a sort of quiet kindness that permeates. Have you ever been to visit a friend at the hospital, and the second you walk out the lobby doors you look around and see the world just a little bit differently? You feel a mixture of relief, sadness, and optimism. The experience produces a shift in perspective. You feel happy to be alive, grateful for what you have, and in a more giving and forgiving mood.

Indeed, studies confirm that people are more charitable and forgiving after they have spent some time contemplating their own mortality.[5] Therefore, be alert for any such opportunity to try to make peace with the person you wronged. It doesn't have to be something sad, but rather any significant event—be it a birth or death, a wedding or a divorce—that brings a little perspective into his life. During these critical life-cycle moments, our values and priorities become realigned, and this provides the opportunity to open the gateways of communication. Any action—a phone call, card, gift, or something, anything—gives you a chance to reconnect and pave the way for a resolution.

If, over time, we make several attempts at reconciliation yet continue to meet with great resistance, then it might be necessary for us to move on. The quality of any relationship is determined by the one who wants it the least, not the most. But there's a difference between someone not *wanting* to forgive and someone who is *uninterested* in having any type of relationship. If the other person has no interest in reconciling, perhaps it's best to let things be. If, however, the other person's hurt feelings are too intense for him to move past them now, we should revisit the situation after a few months or a year, depending on what happened, and try again. Because in this instance, it's the freshness of the pain, rather than a lack of desire to reconcile, that impedes reconciliation. If we still meet with resistance, remember that *we can only give away what we have.* If we want to be forgiven, we may need to forgive others. If we hold on to ill will over what someone has done to us, we can't be authentic with the person we have injured. If we can resolve any anger we're sustaining—be it toward ourselves or toward another person—we will find a smoother path ahead to achieving peace in the current situation.

PART V

HOW TO LOVE BEING ALIVE

16
A Date with Destiny

Although we shouldn't preoccupy ourselves with thoughts of our demise, the only way we can live with intellectual honesty is to acknowledge that one day the sun will rise and set without us in this world. If we find this depressing, rather than motivating, we are not alone. In truth, we belong to the overwhelming majority.

The approaching threat of death as a positive motivator has zero traction in the lives of those who have no life. On the contrary, thinking of death doesn't make them want to live, but, rather, they welcome their final exit, so that they can permanently escape. Dr. Dean Ornish, Harvard professor and president of the Preventive Medicine and Research Institute, writes:

> People may initially get interested in changing their lifestyle because they are hurting, but what sustains these changes is not fear of dying, it's joy of living. . . . What often lies at the root of self-destructive behaviors is loneliness, depression, and isolation. The number-one epidemic in America is not obesity or heart disease, it is depression. The most commonly prescribed prescription drugs last year were antidepressants. We assume that people want to live longer, but telling somebody that they will live longer

if they just quit smoking and change their diet is not very motivating if they feel depressed, stressed out, and unhappy.

People are trying to kill themselves because they want to die, and being informed that their actions will hasten their death incentivizes self-destructive behavior. When death is not a deterrent, it doesn't stop their self-destructive behavior and only incites their insolence in regard to life.

THE KEY TO SELF-CONTROL

A well-lived life gives meaning to death, and in exchange, death gives renewed meaning to life. Therefore, the constructive power of contemplating death is in force only when we appreciate life itself, and our lives in particular. Otherwise, we experience no real shift in our mind-set; we just slide along the spectrum to another shade of gray. Coupons have an expiration date to force us to act, but if we're not interested in the products, then the coupons are just as useless to us before the date as they are after the date.

Having purpose in our lives gives us a broader perspective on life *and* on death. This is crucial, because a pivotal factor in our ability to exercise self-control lies in how we manage our fears. *Terror management theory* explains that we deal with the fear of death and the resultant anxiety in one of two ways. When we live full, robust lives, we tend to embrace our values and beliefs— whatever brings meaning into our lives. Known as the *mortality salience hypothesis*, it promotes self-regulation. Alternatively, if we already have one foot in the Land of Escapism, we are inclined to pacify our fears by further indulging ourselves—in anything from chocolate to extravagant vacations. This is known as the *anxiety buffer hypothesis*. For this reason, stories on the news relating to disaster and death make viewers respond more positively to advertisements for status products, such as luxury cars and designer clothes.[1]

A shrinking world compounds our prospects for experiencing emotional distress because *terror management* is no longer confined to our own lives and experiences. Thanks to the technological age, our brains must process a confounding number of calamities and catastrophes—all of which we log and lodge as clear and present dangers. In the days of our ancestors, or even through a good portion of the 1900s, by the time one heard the news, it was not news anymore; our forebears' senses were not constantly overwhelmed with photos and videos of every natural or manmade disaster that took place within the past twenty minutes. We are too easily overloaded by all the horrors we witness via technology—right in our living rooms, bedrooms, or even cars. As we become aware of the myriad mishaps and misfortunes happening all around us, our brains react as if we're experiencing them in real time.

The dry cough that turns out to be lung cancer for 1 in 3.5 million nonsmokers becomes the source of incessant worry because we "know so many people" who had such a diagnosis. We turn away from the statistically improbable in favor of fear because of all of the people "in our lives" whose stomach aches turned out to be a tumor, who were randomly attacked in broad daylight, or who became paralyzed from a mosquito bite. An endless onslaught of unpredictable and unavoidable horrors awaits us at every turn. It's to be expected that neurotic has become the new normal.

THE EVIDENCE

The consequences speak for themselves. An estimated 67 percent of the population is overweight or obese. The result: Cardiovascular disease, cancer, and diabetes account for nearly two of every three deaths in the United States. Sales of antidepressant, antianxiety, and mood-stabilizing drugs have hit record levels, and today, one in four Americans suffers from mental illness (and Americans today are ten times as likely to suffer from depression as they were in the 1960s, even accounting for increased awareness and diagnosis).

Our coping mechanism for physical pain has been similarly compromised. In the United States, the number of prescriptions written for major painkillers rose 90 percent between 2003 and 2011. In total, according to the *New England Journal of Medicine*, 116 million Americans suffer with persistent pain—an astounding 1 out of 3 people. Our tolerance for reality—much less pain of any sort—is crippled.

This crystallizes the crucial necessity to know exactly what we are living for. Nothing other than a clearly defined purpose with meaningful growth will insulate us from the quakes of insanity that would otherwise shake our emotional foundation and force us to flee from reality. Our lives fill with ever-vivid reminders of the true nature of this world. As we snap into heightened awareness, so much seems irrelevant—at least, in the moment. Our soul wants to attach to the one true reality, where we find permanence and meaning. Yet without a sense of purpose in our lives, we don't have the anchor of trust, and without this unspoken assurance, we shift to a mentality of "Let us eat and drink; for tomorrow we shall die." The Achilles' heel of anger control—the foundational trigger of all susceptibility—lies in how we manage our fears.

17
Becoming Extraordinary

King Solomon tells us throughout Ecclesiastes that all suffering comes from trying to give permanence to the temporary. The soul seeks permanence through giving—investing in a commodity that is forever ours. It recognizes that we keep whoever we become, and that is ultimately shaped by what we give, not by what we take. Our soul is drawn to reunite with Immortality, but the aberration of this quest is the ego's search for permanence through taking. The ego lunges after longevity through influence, power, and control, while the soul yearns for true independence—freedom over the lower self—that enables the apex in self-expression.

The ego relishes creative acts in order to make its mark on the world—an illogical pursuit of monuments and awards, anything that will stand the test of time. (It's illogical because even while the person rejects a world beyond this one, he desires to be remembered. But why? If he has no existence beyond the physical world, why should he care whether people who come after him are aware of accomplishments? What good does this do him? None, according to his own logic, but his soul knows differently.) Our ego thirsts to be special, desperately longing to set itself apart, even if it tears us apart. It doesn't care whether the goal is accomplished through productive or destructive means. It seeks only to make a big splash.

Ironically, the ego chase leaves us with a homogenized, blended existence that merely blurs our uniqueness. When we follow a destructive path in a futile attempt to be different, we end up as carbon copies of all other ego-oriented people and are confined to an automated existence and a generic personality. When our ego dominates, our lives are indeed programmed—but we are the programmers.

When a person stays busy building an image or succumbing to cravings and impulses, he never rises above reactionary living. He doesn't create anything—certainly not himself. When we are independent, we are partners in our own creation and in creation itself, exercising the height of free will. The desire to create burns deep within us. We derive intense, unparalleled satisfaction from creative thought and action. They rivet our attention and unleash our individuality. We notice how much pleasure a small child receives from drawing a picture. We are driven to be unique, to express ourselves.

WHO ARE YOU LIVING FOR?

There is no status quo in nature. The law of conservation states that organisms die if they don't grow. Moreover, just as every person is one of a kind—from his fingerprints to his face to his DNA—we are all born with a specific purpose, unique to each one of us. To obtain the highest level of fulfillment, we must move toward that which our soul desires—which Maslow explains as self-transcendence, to go beyond the ego. Too often, we confine our options to a small space, not fully recognizing the range of possibilities that extends beyond our comfort zone. Our egos lead us to believe that we are boxed in and can't go beyond our circumstances, or can move only a little, gradually. Lack of inspiration really amounts to lack of enthusiasm for the direction, speed, and distance that we believe we can move.

To become reenergized, we need to expand our thinking. Saying *I hate my life* doesn't produce an answer that moves us forward. It's not even a question, but a statement that reinforces our complacency. We must open ourselves up to the field of possibilities by asking ourselves, *What do I want out of life?* The following additional questions nudge the ego out of the equation and help us to further crystalize our thinking. When you ask yourself these questions, give thought to what answer satisfies most of them or, even better, all of them.

1. What would you do if you could not fail?

2. What would you do if you didn't have the problems that you have?

3. What would you do if you had all the money that you ever needed?

4. What would you do if no one would ever find out/if everyone would find out?

Check your motivation. We must be honest about *why* we want what we want. So many people feel miserable because they set goals based on someone else's expectations. They had every reason to do what they did, except for the right reason: Because they considered it important for their own growth and to create the future they truly wanted.

ARE WE ALL ON THE SAME PAGE?

Living in a way that contradicts our core values and soul-inspired passion drains us because it creates a division within us. No reasonable parent would consider selling his or her child for any sum of money, but this same parent might spend very little time with that child. We cannot simultaneously value X as all-important, then spend our time, energy, and effort on a goal Y, without creating an internal tug of war. Equally vital is that the totality of our goals are compatible amongst themselves, in addition to being aligned with our values. Renowned psychoanalyst Karen Horney writes,

> We have to make sure our goals are synergistic—living with unresolved conflicts involves primarily a devastating waste of human energies, occasioned not only by conflicts themselves but by all the devious attempts to remove them. When a person is basically divided he can never put his energies wholeheartedly into anything, but wants always to pursue two or more incompatible goals. This means he will either scatter his energies or actively frustrate his efforts. . . . [N]o matter how potentially gifted he is—[his efforts] will be wasted. . . . Divided energies also cause him to unconsciously rebel and insist on perfection, forgetfulness, overworking, etc., neurotic inertia is a paralysis of initiative and action.[1]

Other findings share this conclusion and reveal that people with conflicting goals worry more and get less done. They also have "fewer positive emotions, more negative emotions and more depression and anxiety . . . Even just plain physical sickness was higher among the people with conflicting goals. The more the goals conflicted, the more the people got stuck, and the more un-happy and unhealthy they became."[2]

In the gap between where we are and where we want to be, we find instability—the breeding ground of anger. Three intersecting reasons are involved: First, the extent to which we live responsibly and meet our obligations—in accordance with the soul, rather than ego—shapes our initial perspective. It determines our entire worldview, because the ego forms false or unhealthy beliefs and values to protect us, based on our limitations. Second, when we have self-respect, we optimize our relationships and interpersonal interactions: we don't take things personally; we forgive and apologize with ease; we see others' points of view; we are not prone to anger or offense or inclined to jealousy or envy; we can empathize, see the good in others, and judge favorably; and certainly, we don't need to be right. Third, the more frustrated we feel with ourselves and in our lives, the more readily we become annoyed by others. Indeed, the person who is going nowhere in life often seems the most bothered by slow-moving traffic.

18

Escaping the Trap of Procrastination

Living one's life with authenticity—meaningful goals aligned with our values—allows us to overcome the single greatest obstacle to moving our lives forward in a significant, purposeful direction: procrastination. Let's see how this is so.

Scattered or misdirected ambition is as debilitating as inactivity itself. Movement is useless without a plan—we need a place to go and a path to get there. We must not live our lives like the person who shoots an arrow at the side of a barn and then draws a circle around it after it embeds itself. Caring little about what he aims for, he proudly convinces himself and the world that he has succeeded. Many people indeed feel reluctant to plan their lives. They might have a vague idea of what they want to accomplish, yet they shy away from preparing for their future. This is true for two interlacing reasons.

What exactly does planning for the future involve? At the most elementary level, we must acknowledge where we are and then decide where we want to go. The challenge here exists as much in the first half of this process as in the second. Yes, the future holds many unknowns and uncertainties, but our hidden fear lies in not wanting to see where we are. We are afraid to examine our lives too closely and to come face-to-face with who we have become, and with what happened to our finest intentions. The reluctance to set goals and plan for the future relieves us of the burden of self-examination. However, another deep-seated constraint exists.

To move forward, we need to weigh different possibilities and directions our lives can take. To do this, we must know what we are living for. In other words, we must commit. Yet we would rather get lost in the grand scheme of daydreaming than be forced to make choices that will forever define who we are. (It's interesting that the English word *decide* has the same etymological root as *homicide*: the Latin word *cadre*, meaning "to cut down" or "to kill.") But we half believe that if we never make a choice, we won't have to live with failure or regret. Functional magnetic resonance imaging (fMRI) has shown that when we make decisions couched in uncertainty, it stimulates the amygdala—the "fear and anxiety response center." Our brains are literally afraid of being wrong.[1] So rather than move our lives forward, we leave ourselves open to every possibility, with the misplaced hope that the perfect opportunity will present itself. And don't think that our intelligence or talent shields us against the crime of procrastination. On the contrary, intelligent people can always find endless rationales that support different courses of action.

It's human nature to want to keep our options open, and as the ego looms larger, it magnifies the fear of commitment—we can't fail, be wrong, or feel restricted. It always looks for a way out, should we want to escape. Yet the ego built this back door out of fear, and indecision doesn't free us, it keeps us trapped and bends us into someone who is afraid to live. Nothing will become of our lives—NOTHING—until we decide what we want out of life and are prepared to make a profound commitment to that decision. If we don't recognize this truth, we can't go any further.

THE ANTIDOTE: AN AUTHENTIC SELF

People typically rank public speaking as their number-one fear. Death ranks at number two. To eliminate jitters associated with public speaking, one need only focus on the audience and their needs. We cannot be self-conscious if we are not thinking about ourselves. When the speaker's thoughts are geared toward others, he moves from taking to giving. And where there is no ego, there is no anxiety. If the speaker is consumed with how he is going to come across—*Will they like me? Will I make a fool of myself?*—he can't help but become nervous. In our own lives, the greater the difference between the image we wish to project and our true self, the greater the fear.

As we previously discussed, living authentically allows the false identity to dissolve because its only purpose is to keep you from seeing yourself. At this point your fears dissolve. We go after what we want without the reins of self-doubt, because when it's not about us, we can access any trait we need, to accomplish what we wish. When there is no ego, we can rise above any fear; and when there is no fear, there is no delay. To keep an irrational quest for perfection from becoming an excuse for procrastination and a source of unrelenting anger and frustration, you have to get real with who you are—only then can you fearlessly pursue what you want.

In the words of Emerson, "To be yourself in a world that is constantly trying to make you something else is the greatest accomplishment." When our goals are tainted by the ego, we play it safe and convince ourselves that we're playing it smart; but we aren't living life, we're hiding from ourselves. The only fear we should occupy ourselves with is the failure to actualize our God given abilities, because shame lives in the home of unrealized potential.

PART VI

RECLAIMING OURSELVES AND REDEFINING OUR BOUNDARIES

19
Redrawing the Lines with Boundary Breachers

If you want to live anger free, then you've got to know who you are, be who you are, and stand up for who you are. So, here we are again, back to talking about relationships. When it comes to unleashing our most base nature, no area in life tries us more than our relationships. And while we can cultivate character in serenity and solitude, the true measure of our greatness and growth—where the rubber meets the road—is in the domain of relationships.

It is therefore the height of arrogance to presume that if all of the difficult people in our lives would simply disappear, we would be more productive, happier, and more successful. We bemoan these emotional vampires who drain our life's blood and exhaust our time, money, and energy, but these relationships provide the necessary soil for us to develop our full potential. Putting the spiritual component aside, however, we must remind ourselves of the inexorable link between our mental health and the quality of our relationships. As was discussed earlier, a person with low self-esteem has difficulty maintaining healthy relationships. Yet equally compelling is that even the healthiest among us have to beware, because people in our lives with low self-esteem can wear on our emotional heath, despite our best efforts to work on ourselves.

If we learn how to navigate these relationships, it will go a long way toward preserving our sanity and our ability to maintain our calm.

GOOD FENCES MAKE GOOD NEIGHBORS

Because the quality of our relationships and our mental health are intertwined, boundaries are not simply a nice idea, but integral to the totality of our well-being. Poor boundaries may lead to a breakdown not only of the relationship but of the individual—of ourselves—as well. Unless and until we establish proper boundaries, we are allowing other people, who are quite possibly unwell, to define us and the relationship.

A poor self-image often translates into porous borders—because if a person does not have a clear definition of himself, he is unable to recognize what is proper between him and others. This may manifest as the chronically needy person who asks to be rescued from every self-made crisis; or as the controlling, pushy personality who hides his insecurities with arrogance and bravado. Healthy boundaries are not created to keep people out, but rather to define our space and our sense of personal responsibility.

If someone in your life suffers from an emotional illness, recognize that you cannot make it your life's work to cure the person or even to educate him, because this is most likely not even within your ability. Instead, you should focus on maximizing the potential of the relationship. Certainly, to the degree that someone can accept constructive criticism, you have an obligation to help him see the consequences of his behavior, but only if you feel that you might succeed.

Once you come to terms with the reality of his condition and his limitations, you'll find it easier to accept this person into your life. Still, just because two people are related or have contact with each other doesn't necessarily mean they have a relationship—at least not in the traditional, healthy sense. A genuine relationship involves two people who give and take. Yet if the other person is incapable of giving, then our expectations will routinely exceed the limits of his ability—and we will always feel frustrated.

Apart from immediate family, if, instead, we reframe the dynamics and consider it *kindness*, then we won't rely on him to reciprocate our efforts or fulfill his obligations according to the definition of a normal relationship. Our mind-set largely depends on our expectations. How we frame our interactions greatly affects our attitude toward a person. It is essential to requalify this guidance because when it comes to immediate family members, we can't simply recuse ourselves of our obligations by redefining the relationship and calling it something else. Although we can't let unwell people draw the boundary lines, for our own emotional health, we must make every effort to maintain the best working relationship possible.

THE SHAPE OF THINGS TO COME

In certain instances, we must say, "Enough is enough." Yet we shouldn't believe that the larger solution means cutting difficult people out of our lives. Rarely is this required. Only when we react to another's cruelty with similar behavior do we move to a mode of dependence, and to suffering. Recall our overarching theme: We must act and interact responsibly by moving the ego out of the way. That's it. If we act out of anger, we will suffer. We cannot get around this. Guilt and shame will seep in, our ego deploys to fortify our response, and all the while, our self-esteem and emotional well-being slowly melt.

In our own lives, we know that we don't often feel complete when we feud with, or become estranged from, a member of our immediate family. If, however, we do everything that we can, when we can, for as long as we can, to have the healthiest relationship possible, and it's still not enough, then we may experience sadness over the broken state of the relationship, but we remain whole—emotionally and spiritually intact, undivided by guilt, shame, or resentment. In no way does this mean that we become a doormat and welcome every intolerable person into our lives. Ego negation means that we bring our true self out and into our relationships, with the singular goal of taking responsibility and being responsible. Whether that takes us deeper into or further away from a particular relationship is not at issue. Doing the responsible thing is. Our willingness to do what is legitimately required to foster healthy relationships ultimately gives us peace—allows us to remain whole—regardless of the outcome. Moreover, each time we rise above our nature for the sake of peace, we fortify our wholeness, because all acts of giving refresh our emotional reserves and boost our self-esteem.

TRUE PEACE

True peace does not mean the absence of difference, but the symphony of unique expression. If we forcibly diminish our individuality, this doesn't produce peace—it produces problems. We might easily acquiesce when we subjugate ourselves, but inevitably resentment builds and relationships suffer.

Seeking peace doesn't mean that we let people push past the boundaries of acceptability. At times, the right thing to do is not remaining silent, but to speak up—and stand up—for ourselves and what is right. An obligation to the truth at times supersedes a transient peace, and we can't default to a position of wholesale compliance when common sense dictates that our voice be heard and our position be known—even when it will cause friction. Authentic peace without truth is an oxymoron. It doesn't exist, and those who would recklessly or sheepishly sacrifice the truth will lose both truth and peace—and instead be full of anger and resentment.

20
How to Talk to People Who Don't Listen

"But he's smart! Successful! Talented!" All of this is irrelevant. We must not confuse intelligence with emotional health. As was discussed in Chapter 5, in any given situation, a smart person can make a poor decision, while his less-intelligent counterpart might make a wiser, more thoughtful choice. Our self-esteem, not our intelligence, determines the *direction* of our behavior. An intelligent person has the *potential* to make better choices, but his *motivation* and *capability* to do so are determined by his perspective or emotional health.

The egocentric person will often pride himself on his instincts because he will routinely disregard logic (though he paradoxically sees himself as a man of intellect). He's someone who says, "You have to go with your gut" and "Trust your intuition, no matter what." When the facts invariably conflict with his position we wonder, *How can he be so foolish?* We're looking for the logic behind a rationale that doesn't exist, reason in a psychological landscape devoid of reason. If we become frustrated because someone else simply doesn't get it, we're behaving even more irrationally than he is. The other person can't help himself, but we know better and can choose to end this exercise in futility.

We would do well to abandon the belief that we are only one

perfectly crafted sentence away from showing this person reality—that he is wrong and we are, in fact, right. We often persist in believing that if we just present a rational argument and explain the facts clearly and logically, the other person cannot draw anything other than the right conclusion and will then see things our way—the right way. It's similar to an individual who, when conversing with someone who doesn't know his language, speaks slower and louder, enunciating each word and making animated facial expressions. On one level, he recognizes that the other person doesn't understand a single word that he utters, but his emotional self cannot fathom how this can be, when the words seem so clear to him.

When dealing with someone like this, we need to muster up as much empathy as possible. Such a person is disconnected from his true self—the soul—and from others, and suffers from intense feelings of loneliness, regardless of the crowds around him. As we explained in Chapter 3, his inability to connect with others is extremely painful and isolating. Moreover, despite what we may want to believe, this person probably doesn't wake up in the morning with the thought, *How can I make your life miserable today?* Hurt people hurt. Not because they are bad, but because they are in pain. Though we all bear responsibility for our behavior, we must not assume a conscious intent in others (and if the behavior is conscious, all the more reason to have empathy, because this person is quite unwell).

DEALING WITH BOUNDARY BREACHERS

Boundaries are not selfish—they are responsible. We need to establish healthy boundaries to give the relationship a chance to survive and perhaps even to thrive. Moreover, our efforts help the person become more self-aware and prevent him from doing psychological harm to himself. How? Because it damages him emotionally every time he takes advantage of us, and it reinforces his corrupted thought process, not to mention the quality of the relationship.

Because of porous boundaries, he will try to take things that don't belong to him without compunction—our time, our energy, our attention—in much the same way that a thief would take our money or possessions. We need to remember that words are rarely enough, and we will find it futile, time and again, to merely state, *Please do not cross this boundary.* The same applies to physical boundaries. If we don't want someone to break into a sensitive area, such as private building, we put up a fence and install an alarm; we might even remind the would-be thief that trespassing is a punishable crime—and spell out the exact penalty. We wouldn't, however, put up a sign that says, DO NOT STEAL. Those who respect boundaries don't need it, and those who do not won't respect the sign.

To set boundaries with unhealthy people, we cannot tell them what to do. Rather, we must tell them how we'll respond if they breach our boundaries. To be certain, we don't have to convey this harshly or bluntly—to the contrary. With kindness and compassion, we want to explain our boundaries and the consequences for violating them with unacceptable behavior.

DRAW THE LINE AND STAY STRONG

Low self-esteem will make us wary of confrontation, fearing that we will be rejected or abandoned; but we can't shy away from being responsible because someone might be upset with us. He probably will act irrationally (and become angry) if we don't do what he wants (which is, in fact, irresponsible). We cannot, though, give in to his demands (and act irresponsibly) to prevent him from acting irresponsibly. Do you see the lunacy of this? It is sheer foolishness and utterly pointless for us to deviate from behaving responsibly simply because someone will get angry at us if we do. We cannot allow another individual to force us to do something that is wrong merely because he'll respond unreasonably if we do what is right. In that case, not only would we be acting irresponsibly to avoid his anger, we'd end up getting angry with ourselves and become resentful toward him.

As we explore the psychological dynamics more closely, we find that what really bothers us is that we get bothered; what really annoys us is that we get annoyed. If we become angry—or act otherwise negligently—we move to a state of dependency, because someone "causes" us to respond in a way that we do not choose. Unpleasant circumstances in general, and difficult people in particular, push us toward an irrationally charged reaction. Choosing to respond calmly, irrespective of our negative emotional state, epitomizes mental health. Whatever such a person asks of us, we either say, "Yes," with joy or "No," calmly and guilt free. Giving in out of fear or guilt does nothing to enhance our self-esteem. To the contrary, giving in diminishes it. Such a situation is not really giving; it is the other person taking.

You probably know from your own life experiences that when someone tries to guilt you into doing something and you stand up for yourself—just say *no*—you feel better about yourself. You also experience a similar empowerment when you say *yes* to a request that you believe you should accommodate, even if you aren't in the mood. The bottom line is that whatever you say or do, if it's from a position of strength—that is, *you choose* your course of action—you will infuse yourself with an unwavering sense of self-respect.

21
Speak Now, or Forever Be in Pieces

In learning how to express ourselves, it's useful to be aware of our usual modus operandi, or method of operating. People respond to conflict in one of five ways: (1) by accepting it; (2) by retreating from it; (3) by surrendering to it or suppressing it; (4) by fighting; or (5) by shutting down.

Acceptance is the healthiest response. This person sees and accepts the situation for what it is and doesn't become angry or allow his emotions to dictate his response. Rationally and objectively, he weighs the options and then fortifies his decision with the necessary emotional weight. *Retreat* is typical of passive-aggressive individuals, who withdraw to avoid confrontation. The passive-aggressive person lacks the confidence and courage to face the situation head on, so he backs down in the moment, but gets back at the person in another way, at another time. His retaliation, or revenge, may take the form of being late, "forgetting" to do something important for the other person, or just generally inconveniencing the other person in some way.

The person who *surrenders* his anger simply gives up and gives in, a response that often reflects codependency and a doormat or compliant personality type. He doesn't feel worthy enough to stand up for himself and/or feels incapable of advancing his own agenda, needs, and wishes. If he is not conscious of these thoughts then he *suppresses* his anger and is unaware that it is eating him up inside; in fact, he may declare—to both himself and to others—to be a very calm and easygoing person who just "rolls with things," and doesn't get too ruffled (while the anger manifests into myriad physiological and emotional issues). The distinction between this class and the passive-aggressive is that the latter doesn't feel entitled to assert himself while the former does, but feels unable to do so directly. The fourth potential response, *fighting*, produces direct, unhealthy conflict. This person, emotionally charged and enraged, chooses to battle it out head-on without the benefit of composure and reason. Finally, if one's emotional state is fragile and the circumstance too overwhelming, he may shut down in an attempt to shut out the pain.

EXPRESS YOURSELF

Whether we are the type to convey our anger passively or openly—or to swallow it or wallow in it—we must learn to express ourselves in a way that optimizes how the other person will hear what we say. As we discussed, we want to approach the person with humility and respect, and calmly communicate how we feel without necessarily assigning blame or assuming a malicious intent. Most importantly, we have to say something! The single biggest killer in any relationship is resentment. Resentment is frozen anger from the past that continues to rear its head. When something distresses us, and we can't deal with it on our own in a healthy way, then it's time to do something; because if we don't speak up when necessary, we may act out in inappropriate ways.

Need a little help asserting yourself? Here's a simple technique from cutting-edge research, and in an upcoming chapter we'll learn an additional strategy to radically transform our self-concept to become more confident, which makes it considerably easier to assert ourselves.

Research out of Harvard University has found a direct correlation between body language and the release of hormones. For both men and women, higher levels of testosterone increase feelings of confidence, while lower levels of cortisol (the stress hormone) reduce anxiety and improve your ability to deal with stress. In just two minutes of maintaining a high-power pose—which is open and relaxed—hormone levels shift dramatically, with a 20 percent increase in testosterone and a 25 percent decrease in cortisol.[1] The Wonder Woman stance is a good example of the power pose: Stand with feet apart, hands on hips, shoulders back. Holding this stance for just two minutes offers immediate results, because you will be physiologically primed and inclined to assert yourself with greater ease; and practicing this pose several times a day can increase our confidence levels in the long-term. Because the research is new, conflicting findings question the extent of hormonal fluctuations, but what remains certain are the multitude of studies with unanimous agreement that such postures and poses have a direct impact on mood and produce a wide range of near-instantaneous cognitive and behavioral changes. For example, in one such experiment, subjects were randomly assigned to adopt one of two postures—either slumped in their seat or sitting straight up—while filling out a mock job application. Asked for an honest self-evaluation, those in the latter group rated themselves more competent and capable than their slouching counterparts.[2]

UNFREEZING RESENTMENT

There's a right and a wrong way to express ourselves, and our approach can make all the difference in the world. As we know for ourselves, sometimes we're more open, and other times, the slightest critical comment can send us crawling under the nearest rock or make us defensive and argumentative. *What* we say, *how* we say it, *where* we say it, and *when* we say it will influence how other people receive our comments. The following ten steps will help ensure that we express our words in the optimum ego-free manner, so that people hear them in the kindest way.

If, despite our best efforts, we know the person will become defensive and angry with us, a great technique is to preface our words with something like this: "I'd like to talk with you about an important issue, but I'm concerned that you might get upset with me for bringing it up." Usually, curiosity will get the better of him, and he will assure you that he won't get angry. Believe it or not, this assurance will likely hold true, because his ego won't want him to feel foolish by going back on his word.

According to research, people who are in a good mood are more likely to purchase a lottery ticket.[3] When we are joyful, we tend to be more optimistic and are open to possibilities.[4] Try not to allow your desire to speak your mind derail your ability to successfully plan your approach. Wait until you're both in a positive mood, so you both have the capacity to *give*. When we're in a bad mood or constricted state, we are only capable of taking, making it difficult to see the situation from the other person's perspective. When either one or both of you are hungry, tired, or plainly angry, do not expect that you will have a productive conversation. It's not going to happen too often, if ever.

TEN STEPS TO EGO-FREE COMMUNICATION

1. They Don't Care What You Know, Till They Know That You Care

Without making a big deal about it, let the other person know you're saying this because you *care*—you care about *him* and your *relationship.* There is an age-old maxim: "Words that come from the heart enter the heart." Indeed, only a sincere and heart-felt expression of feelings—and more so, criticism—has a chance of being effective. If you communicate your genuine concern for, and interest in, this person and your relationship with him, he'll receive your words the way you intended.

2. Privacy, Please

Always express yourself in private. Even if you feel that he wouldn't mind others hearing your comments, do it behind closed doors.

3. Always Begin with Praise

First, emphasize the person's many good qualities and remarkable potential, to pave the way for him to hear your point with equanimity. When this person knows that you have genuine respect and appreciation for him—perhaps even reverence or awe—then he'll hear your comments in a way that doesn't engage his ego. For instance, "You're one of the most productive employees, and I'm continually in awe of how you do what you do. I was just wondering about . . ."

4. Depersonalize the Impact

Comments and critiques should address the *act,* not the person. In other words, instead of saying, "You're incompetent or reck-less," it's better to say, "You're such a wonderful person, and this behavior doesn't seem suited to someone of your principled character."

5. Accidents Happen
Don't assume or insinuate that this behavior is something that he's doing knowingly, consciously, or deliberately. If the situation allows, approach it as something he's doing unwittingly, or even unconsciously.

6. We're In This Together
Share some of the *responsibility*, if you can. The approach of shared responsibility makes it you and him against this "thing"—*not you against him.* You might say something like, "I should have been more specific when we covered this." This approach is, of course, more effective than "I hate it when you . . ." Or try, "I'm having a hard time when you . . ." rather than, "You have no right to . . ." or "Because you don't care enough . . ."

7. Identify the Problem, and Put Energy into the Solution
Expressing ourselves can be both empowering and cathartic, even when the other person is unable to fully understand what we're saying or how we're feeling. But if we are speaking out only to correct this person's behavior, then we want to be solution-oriented. If there is no answer, then you should never have brought it up in the first place, because it serves no purpose. And if you believe that no matter what you say, he won't take your advice, then it's also best not to bring it up. If you do, then you only serve your own interests, and you won't help the situation.

8. You're Not Alone

Criticism is most effective when you tell him that he's not alone. If you convey that whatever he has done or is doing is very common (and perhaps even something that you've done yourself), this diffuses the impact on his ego, so that he won't take it so personally. And that's really the reason he might become so offended. When we openly acknowledge our own faults to the person we criticize, our humility then keeps the other's ego from engaging. Conversely, an attitude of self-righteousness will automatically galvanize the other's ego, and he will likely become defensive.

9. Speak Softly and Forget the Stick

Be calm and pleasant. King Solomon stated, "The words of the wise, when spoken gently, are accepted." When these conversations take a turn for the worse, it's got less to do with who's right and who's wrong, and more with the wrong tone of voice. Speaking softly and politely will help the person digest your message in the manner you intend. Relationship expert Dr. John Gottman reports, "Ninety-six percent of the time you can predict the outcome of a conversation based on the first three minutes of the fifteen-minute interaction. A harsh startup dooms you to failure. The rule is, 'If it starts negative, it stays negative.' "[5]

10. Far and Away, Then Bomb's Away

The best time to criticize is *when you are distanced from the event in proximity and in time.* Being removed from the environment and putting *time* between the event and your criticism produce quite different results from speaking up immediately. Although you may verbally assure the person that the criticism is no big deal, you don't convey that attitude by offering your observation in the moment. By waiting a few days, you reduce his ego attachment to the situation, and he feels less sensitive to criticism. But the closer to the event (in both time and proximity) that you criticize, *the more he identifies* with his behavior, and the more defensive he will become.

Expressing our displeasure is, at times, required and beneficial for our emotional and physical health. Yet articulating our feelings isn't the same as unleashing a torrent of unrestrained anger. When an objective assessment dictates that we should speak up, both our emotional health and the relationship can be enhanced. Yet without substance and sincerity—much less calm and composure—our words won't be productive to either the relationship or ourselves. Difficult people are not in our lives to add to our woes but to help us, and we need to realize this, or they will keep coming around again and again—and so we might keep coming around, again and again. On a simple level, it's true that we should help others, but we must also understand the larger picture and ask ourselves the important question: "What lesson can I learn from this person?" While we remain in "blame mode," we are not solution-oriented and therefore can't see, let alone investigate, ways to improve the situation.

Note: Do you still have trouble seeing yourself as a healthy, assertive type? Chapter 24 shows you how to literally rewire your brain not only to control your anger, but also to turn positive assertiveness into your second nature.

22
Successful Relationships with Impossible People

Because our emotional health and the quality of our relationships are intertwined, it's beneficial to do what we can to improve our relationships, even with people who are burdensome. As we learned, this doesn't mean that you have to include every difficult person in every aspect of your life, but to remove your ego from the equation when dealing with such a person. The following principles describe how to change the foundation of a relationship and enhance the way you interact and communicate with another person, whether you are seeking to improve a relationship with a friend, family member, or coworker.

1. R-E-S-P-E-C-T

Aretha Franklin sang the truth! Many personality conflicts arise as a result of someone feeling disrespected. You may have unintentionally not given someone your full attention, or they misinterpreted something you said or did. Although it doesn't take much for a person with low self-esteem to imagine that a person doesn't like them, this is true for all of us, to some degree. There are aspects of ourselves that we dislike, and we project our own disdain with these qualities onto others. We believe (albeit unconsciously) that others must see these faults and dislike us as well.

An effective way to show someone that you hold them in esteem is to tell a third party, maybe a mutual friend, what it is that you genuinely like and respect about this other person. Or you could commend this other person directly for something they have done, or for something they stand for. Once the person sees your admiration, the barriers of hostility will begin to break down. After all, it is hard to dislike someone who not only likes us but also respects us.

Have you ever had the experience of having someone whom you don't particularly like pay you a huge compliment or ask your advice about something? Suddenly you find yourself forced to reevaluate your feelings toward them to something more favorable. We would rather adjust our thinking about someone than believe that their high opinion of us is flawed. This form of appreciation is known as *reciprocal affection*. We tend to like someone once we are told that they have the same feelings for us. To further this, avoid gestures or comments that indicate a lack of respect. Specifically, when someone is speaking to you, give them your undivided attention. Being half-listened to, or more accurately, being half-ignored, does not cultivate warm feelings. Perhaps you've had the experience of conversing with someone at an event when you suddenly become aware that their eyes are roving the room behind you, even as they're listening to you. Listening—really listening—is about respect. It might seem trivial, but this type of consideration for another person's honor significantly impacts a relationship. Imagine having a conversation with someone and their phone rings, but they choose not to answer it. And when you say, "Do you need to get that?" they simply say, "Don't worry about it. I'm only interested in talking to you right now." Wouldn't this make you feel good?

2. Let Them Give to You

We tend to believe that the way to get people to like us is to do nice things for them. Although this is true, people actually like us even more when they do something for us. This is due to the following two reasons: (1) Whenever we invest—time, money, attention—into anything, particularly a person, we care more about and feel more connected to the recipient of our giving. (2) When we allow others to give, they feel better about themselves because giving reinforces the feeling that they are in control and independent.

There is no greater way to bond with someone than by allowing them to be a part of your life and give to you. Ask a person for advice and input whenever you think they might have something worthwhile to contribute.

3. Show Your Human Side

You should never be afraid of responsibly opening up to the people in your life. When you show your vulnerability, a wall between yourself and the other person dissolves, and empathy emerges; that person is then driven to respond to your needs as if they were his own. Often, in an attempt to get someone to like us, we employ what is called *self-enhancement behavior*; this is when we tell and show the other person how accomplished and wonderful we are, so that they will like us. Yet research clearly indicates that when you're dealing with a person who is insecure and feels threatened, self-deprecating behavior is the optimum approach. This would mean that you offer information about yourself that isn't flattering, but this admission shows humility, honesty, and trust—three traits that help provide a successful resolution to any personality conflict.

4. Recognize That Like Attracts Like

Contrary to popular opinion, research in human behavior confirms that opposites do not attract.[1] We may find some people interesting because of how different they are from us, but we actually connect more with people who are similar to us and have similar interests. Analogous to this law is the principle of *comrades in arms*. People who go through life-changing situations together tend to create a significant bond. For instance, soldiers in battle or those in fraternity pledge classes who get hazed together usually develop strong friendships.

It's for this reason that two people who have never met but who have shared a similar previous experience—whether it's an illness or winning the lottery—can become instant friends. When you speak to this person, talk about what you both enjoy and what you have in common.

5. Show Genuine Enthusiasm

Psychologist Daniel Goleman writes: "It happens that smiles are the most contagious emotional signal of all, having an almost irresistible power to make other people smile in return."[2] Smiling at someone not only helps them feel good about themselves, but also makes you feel good about yourself. The importance of immediately setting the right tone at the beginning of a conversation cannot be overstated. In every type of relationship, whether you are returning home to your spouse or greeting a coworker, those initial few moments together will dramatically shape the quality of the rest of your encounter.

6. Say a Few Kind Words

It's unfortunate, but it seems that in many of our relationships, the only time we say something nice is when we've done something wrong. Be proactive from time to time; one kind word in the bank is worth a hundred after the fact. In research examining sixty-nine studies about influencing impressions and getting a person to like us, the most successful tactic was found to be simply making the other person feel good about themselves, whether through a sincere compliment or praise. The bottom line is that people crave feeling good about themselves, and most people are forced to rely on others to sustain them. One terrific and simple way to implement this with those closest to us is to express once or twice a day—via text, email, call, a short note, or in person—your admiration, respect, or appreciation for something specific.

7. Be an Ally

If you learn that someone has made a mistake, reassure them that it could happen to anyone, and tell them they shouldn't be so hard on themselves. Whatever you do, don't criticize or condemn. In a situation where someone is having a disagreement, defend them when you believe there's merit to their side of the argument. And when the two of you have a disagreement, you don't win anything by proving that you're smarter than they are, whereas if you acknowledge that they've made an insightful point, and validate their feelings, you have everything to gain, even if you disagree with them.

8. Either Side of the Aisle

Sometimes the source of conflict is rooted in something deeper: ideals. Objecting to a person's ideology does not usually give you the permission to sever the relationship, or to hate the other person. However, the reason the relationship suffers is the way the two parties treat each other as a result of this divide. Invariably, with each disrespectful comment or disapproving glare, each side feels even more justified in disliking the other. It is this cycle of disrespect that gives way to ingrained hostility. The root of the conflict could be tolerable, even manageable, but because of the charged atmosphere, the two parties often allow their relationship to deteriorate to the point of no return. Even if a great deal of time has gone by, you can still reverse the situation by showing complete respect despite the other's comments and attitude. This method engages two psychological principles:

The first psychological phenomenon is the previously discussed *cognitive dissonance.* If you're treating a person well in spite of how badly they're treating you, then they have to reconcile why they're being rude and intolerant to somebody who is kind and respectful. To resolve the contradiction, they will often be forced to conclude that you must be a good person who holds a flawed belief, rather than a bad person who should be ignored. The second psychological phenomenon is *guilt reduction.* Studies show that a person will do almost anything to eliminate feelings of guilt. When you're treating another person kindly but they're treating you poorly, they will, on some level, feel guilty. In order to reconcile these feelings, they will be inclined to change their behavior and become more tolerant.

Many people have friendships and relationships with people whose beliefs are fundamentally different from their own. The secret is to stay away from contentious subjects. Not every issue needs a thorough, complete, and intensive investigation. If you want to find something else to argue about, you will have no shortage of topics.

PART VII

ADVANCED PSYCHOLOGICAL STRATEGIES TO LIVE ANGER FREE

23
The Power of Neuroplasticity

In the middle of a taxing circumstance, we might find it difficult to present a composed demeanor—let alone to feel calm. But little by little, our capacity to do so develops. By choosing a different response to anger now, we can better control ourselves the next time we feel provoked.

For many years, conventional thinking likened the mind to a steam kettle, in which pressure would build until the lid blew off. Psychologists thus encouraged people to release the buildup of pressure by venting their anger. Yet after extensive research on the subject, it turns out that expressing anger is not only unproductive, but also destructive. "When people vent their feelings aggressively they often feel worse, pump up their blood pressure, and make themselves even angrier."[1] Multiple experiments confirm that fits of rage are more likely to intensify anger.[2] This happens because we unconsciously validate our reaction by convincing ourselves that the situation requires our emotionally charged response. In turn, our anger flares, and our self-justification increases our aggression. When we hold on to anger, we suffer; and the more we unleash it, the more it consumes us.

The name given to this phenomenon, *facial feedback hypothesis*, extends to all physical expressions (and falls under the principle of embodied cognition, which posits that thought is not merely influenced by physiology, but actually originates from it). In a series of studies, researchers asked subjects to look at disgusting images while hiding their emotions or while holding pens in their mouths in such a way to prevent them from frowning. A third group was given no instructions and told to react naturally. As expected, the subjects who restrained their emotional expression reported feeling less disgusted afterward than control subjects did.[3] Our minds, seeking to reconcile our behavior with our emotional state, conclude that how we express ourselves must be a result of how we feel about the situation (or about whatever behavior we're engaging in).

The tenet that our external actions mold our emotional world is at the root of the psychological principle that "the outward act awakens the internal" and "minds are shaped by deeds." Aristotle is quoted as saying, "We acquire virtues by first having put them into action." Today, *behavior therapy* (also referred to as *behavior modification therapy*) is built on just such an approach. This type of therapy focuses on changing undesirable behaviors by identifying and substituting them with more positive and healthier behaviors. Not only is the symptom being treated, but the behavior modification can also alter the person's personality from the outside in.

MIND YOUR BRAIN

We are born with only two primal fears: the fear of falling and the fear of a loud, startling noise. Every other fear is learned. Our emotional response to any situation can be rerouted—for better or for worse. We find an apt illustration in PTSD (post-traumatic stress disorder), a severe anxiety disorder that can develop after a psychological trauma. A person who returns from war, for example, can suffer from such acute PTSD that the sound of a helicopter or a slamming door may cause sudden panic—because the brain has literally rewired itself, based on a false conclusion. In such instances, adrenaline hijacks the brain and redirects the perceived threat from the prefrontal cortex (the thinking brain) to the amygdala (the fear and anxiety response center). This fear-based disorder bears a striking similarity to an instinctive angry reaction. In the latter, our ego identifies a threat to our emotional selves, rather than to our physical selves, and we don't think, we just react.

Recent discoveries in molecular biology provide us with an understanding of the connection between behavior and circuits of the brain. While the mind creates emotional reactions, these are reinforced in the brain. For instance, if we become upset at someone who treats us impolitely, we will likely react more strongly the next time we encounter a similar situation, because the neural connection between rude people and our anger has been strengthened.

Whatever we repeat strengthens the neuronal connections—whether practicing a musical instrument, becoming angry, or remaining calm. Every brain cell (neuron) adapts to its surroundings—or, more precisely, to the signals the neuron receives from neighboring cells. When two neurons fire repeatedly at the same time, this reinforces the connection between them. Hence, the common idiom in biology: "Neurons that fire together wire together." In fact, this proves true for both emotional and physical responses to stimuli, as a study in *Psychology Today* explains:

Just like muscles, brain circuits grow stronger when we use them—great when you're learning to play the piano, but terrible in the case of a constantly aching joint. "Pain pathways are like a trail in the forest," says Gavril Pasternak, director of molecular neuropharmacology at Memorial Sloan-Kettering Cancer Center in New York City. "If you have a path that is already worn, it is easier to follow and it becomes strengthened."

Through the same neurological process that makes you gradually get better at hitting a racquetball or driving a stick shift, your brain "gets better" at perceiving the pain—you become more sensitive and more likely to register a poke or a twinge as painful. Eventually, people with chronic pain disorders such as fibromyalgia (which affects joints and soft tissues) can find even mild sensations agonizing. Imaging studies reveal what's going on: A gentle touch causes brain areas that process pain to react. Similar findings have been reported in people with unexplained chronic lower back pain. It's not a conscious process—it's one way the brain naturally responds to repeated stimulation.[4]

Returning to our immediate discussion, learning a new response—such as remaining calm when in the face of insult or when we feel otherwise disrespected, anxious, or out of control—stimulates the associated neurons to grow extensions (dendrites) to connect with one another. (Dendrites, the branched projections of a neuron, deliver information to and from the cell.) The greater the number of dendrites, the faster and more smoothly we can understand related information and integrate what we learn into our knowledge base. We literally become smarter, more efficient, and more effective in this area. The inverse equally applies. Underused connections gradually deteriorate and eventually fade.[5] Using an electron microscope, we can even see how the inactive connections in the brain gradually disappear.[6] A person can thereby fuel the self-control coffers by maintaining control, or unwittingly deplete his capacity to restrain himself with willful, repeated, prolonged outbursts of rage.

HOW LONG DOES IT TAKE?

Neural pathways are in constant motion. When a blind person compensates for his lack of sight by developing his sense of touch to learn Braille, the borders of the brain begin to realign in just minutes, expanding areas of the cerebral cortex that control the index finger.[7] How long it takes to fully impress a new neural network depends on the intensity, duration, and frequency of both the established routine and the new replacement behavior. Conflicting conclusions exist, in part because we must consider a multitude of factors. Traditionally accepted findings state that constant, repetitive action reconfigures our brains once the neural pathways are bombarded for twenty-one consecutive days. More recent research from the *European Journal of Social Psychology* finds that it takes, on average, sixty-six days of continuous activity to ingrain a new habit into our physiology. Then, with sufficient repetition, the new behavior becomes automatic. Still, other research suggests that the brain requires focused repetition for six months for neuroplasticity to effect complete change, so that we instinctively respond differently. However long it takes, this doesn't mean that we won't experience slipups after this point. Yet it does mean that we will have a physiological advantage in every situation right from the start.

Anger begets anger, and silence begets calm. King Solomon said, "A gentle response turns away anger; a harsh response increases anger."[8] Most people traditionally interpreted this as referring to the person we speak to, but the anger he refers to is also our own. We can retrain our brains by establishing a different meaning for the situation—an intellectual or cognitive approach, in which we ask ourselves, "What does this mean?" and come to the non-ego-oriented reality that we have spoken about in the first several sections. This then resets our emotional response. Another way we can retrain our brains is by forcing ourselves to go beyond aiming for a neutral, calm demeanor, and display the opposite behavior. If you recall the previously mentioned phenomena of *facial feedback hypothesis*, the very act of smiling sends the brain a message that the situation is nonthreatening—not only that it's safe to relax, but also that we're already relaxed. In Chapter 27, we will examine a highly effective application for this: to calm ourselves in the heat of the moment.

24
Change Your Self-Concept, Change Your Life

Self-esteem reflects how we *feel* about ourselves, while the self-concept refers to what we know about ourselves. Up until now, we've focused on increasing self-esteem, but now we'll introduce a way for us to positively reshape the self-concept, and rather than change the lens through which we view ourselves, we'll change *who* we look at.

Researchers posed as safety inspectors and asked homeowners whether they would allow the inspectors to place a large DRIVE CAREFULLY sign in their front yards. Only 17 percent gave permission. Other residents, however, were first approached with a smaller request. The "safety inspectors" asked them to hang a three-inch BE A SAFE DRIVER sign in a window. Nearly all homeowners immediately agreed. A few weeks later, the inspectors asked these homeowners to place the gigantic sign on their front lawns. This same group overwhelmingly agreed—76 percent consented to having the unsightly sign in their front yards.[1] Why the radical discrepancy between the two groups? It's simple: Those who first agreed to the smaller request had reshaped their self-concept and now defined themselves as being serious about driver safety. Therefore, by agreeing to the larger request, they signified their ongoing internal commitment to the cause.

Human beings feel driven to act in accordance with how they see themselves. Like a rubber band, we will stretch only so far before snapping back into our original position. Yet revising our self-concept doesn't happen only through our actions, but via the faculty of imagination. Visualization has an amazing ability to transform us because the subconscious mind can't distinguish between imagination and an actual happening. In fact, neuroscientists have identified which parts of the brain light up when a person has a genuine experience and found that the same regions activate when the person simply imagines the experience.

Visualization is so potent that experiments show it producing changes in the body as well as in the mind.[2] For instance, our muscles gain similar strength whether we actually do an exercise or merely visualize ourselves doing it. One study found that if participants imagine doing finger exercises, their strength increased by an average of 22 percent. By comparison, another test group that actually *physically* did the same regimen increased their strength by an average of 30 percent.[3]

Repetitive action patterns also have long-term neural consequences. Scientists have observed these effects at the cellular and the systemic level, even extending to the motor cortex, the muscles that people imagined exercising, along with related muscles. Sixty studies on the power of mental imagery show that the effect was least significant on strict strength tests, better for motor tasks, and best of all for performance with a mental component—most notably, to exercise control over our anger.[4]

We don't need to wait for a challenging situation to occur and then rely on sheer will to overcome our emotional reaction. If we imagine ourselves responding in a certain way, it reshapes our self-concept and produces the same changes in the brain that the actual behavior does. Mentally rehearsing a calm, patient response, for instance, will help our brain reset itself and can accelerate our ability to maintain self-control, even under the most daunting of circumstances.

We can also benefit by reflecting on actual or imagined instances when we displayed a particular trait. A mental peculiarity called *availability heuristics* shows that people often base their self-concept on availability, or how easily they can bring information to mind. For instance, if we could think of several times when we acted calmly and could recall these events quickly, then we would see ourselves—at that moment—as someone with self-control. However, if we had difficulty recalling ever being in a calm state, we would feel that we characteristically react anxiously or angrily. For this reason, some people have a warped perspective of themselves. They have a computer-like memory for remembering their failures and mistakes in life, so they see themselves as failures. Even if our triumphs far outweigh our mistakes, what we readily remember will dictate how we see ourselves.

We can accomplish something else by using this technique: We can become more at ease in asserting ourselves. By rehearsing those times when we stood up for ourselves and expressed our thoughts in a calm and clear way, our memory will be flush with these scenarios, and our self-concept will shape itself around this persona and prime us to behave in this way. Simply recall five to seven times that you asserted yourself and string them together to create a vivid sixty-second "movie trailer" that you can play in your head several times throughout the day, and at those times when you need a turbo boost of assertiveness.

THE COST AND THE CONSEQUENCES

The most valuable way to use visualization is not simply to up-root individual traits, but to acquire the habit of stopping, think-ing, and feeling the consequences of our conduct—to fully absorb where our choices will lead us. If we want to control our anger, we want to get real. We must recognize what's at stake, and per-mit ourselves to feel the unadulterated pain of the wrong choice—as well as the purity and pleasure of choosing responsibly. As we move beyond rational arguments about long-term costs and ben-efits, it's essential that we immerse ourselves in the travesty of the trade-off and the actual harm to us and to our loved ones.

We need to vividly imagine the painful consequences and be-come realistic about what our behavior has cost us thus far. We must visualize what our lives will look like—in five years, in ten years, or in old age—if we don't change our ways. We should also reflect deeply on how we will feel about ourselves and how dif-ferent our lives can be if we become anger free.

The research is definitive. In his book *We Have Met the Enemy: Self-Control in an Age of Excess,* Daniel Akst writes, ". . . what matters, when it comes to self-control, is not so much willpower as vision—the ability to see the future, so that the long-run consequences of our short-run choices are vividly clear. In that sense, our shortcomings in this arena are really failures of imagination."[5] Drenching ourselves with total aware-ness of the consequences is a powerful remedy for impulsive-ness.[6]

Yet consequences matter to us only if we matter to ourselves. Strategies can help us exercise self-restraint, but the only way to rouse our emotional forces is to remind ourselves that we have a higher, more noble purpose.[7] Reaffirming our core values—knowing what we are living for and who we are (a soul, not a body or an ego)—is the strongest factor in replenishing strength of will.[8]

25
Taking Advantage of the Mind/Body Connection

Anger inhibits our ability to see clearly (because the ego distorts our perspective) and our ability to intellectually process information (due to the impact of elevated cortisol levels). Moreover, coping with any kind of stress depletes our willpower, and a chaotic mind and tense nervous system strain our efforts to maintain our calm, regardless of our finest intentions.[1] Common sense testifies to the conclusion of innumerable studies: The calmer we are in ordinary times, the easier it is for us to control our anger in difficult times. The following physiological factors are highly beneficial in reducing our overall stress and anxiety level.

MEDITATION
One effective way to relax the nervous system is through meditation, which, interestingly, has deep roots in almost every major religion or spiritual practice. While a variety of effective stress-management strategies can help us exercise self-control, meditation has proved to be especially useful, and you can enjoy the dividends remarkably fast.[2] Studies show that people who meditated for about thirty minutes a day for eight straight weeks had noticeable increases in gray-matter density in the prefrontal cortex.

At the same time, MRI brain scans showed a reduction of gray matter in the amygdala, a region responsible for anxiety and stress.

More than one thousand independent scientific studies conducted at two hundred universities and institutions in twenty-seven countries, published in leading scientific journals, attest to the psychological and physiological benefits of meditative practice. Herbert Benson, M.D., a professor of medicine at Harvard Medical School who has authored or coauthored more than 170 papers, reports that frequent meditation reduces the level of anxiety, worry, and unconstructive thoughts and fears, as well as increasing the individual level of happiness.[3] He writes, "Meditation induces a host of biochemical and physical changes in the body collectively referred to as the 'relaxation response.' The relaxation response includes changes in metabolism, heart rate, respiration, blood pressure, and brain chemistry."[4] Other findings show that meditation promotes overall psychological health, with benefits that include enhanced confidence and greater self-control, empathy, and self-actualization, as well as decreased anger in high-intensity situations.[5]

BREATHING MEDITATION IN 5 QUICK AND EASY STEPS

Breathing is most effective because it is among the few biological processes that are involuntary and unconscious and yet, we can easily alter it through conscious thought—thus creating a bridge between the unconscious and the conscious minds. In time, this helps us gain control over untamed and unwelcomed thoughts and feelings. Here are the basic steps:

Step 1: Make the atmosphere conducive. You can step out and feel the warmth of sunlight or go for a darkened room. Look for a quiet and serene place that is completely free of distractions or just from extraneous noise. This could be an extra room in your house, the woods, or anywhere that is tranquil.

Step 2: Take a comfortable position. The traditional cross-legged lotus position is fine but unnecessary. The objective is to be comfortable and to assume a position that will not make your body ache or cause distractions during your breath meditation. The simplest position is to sit in a comfortable chair with your feet flat on the floor, hands resting on your lap or armrests.

Step 3: Start by slowly breathing in through your nose and out through your mouth. Each breath in should be held for about four to six seconds and then slowly released. Be mindful of your breath, how it feels as you inhale, then as you hold it, and then as you slowly exhale. After five minutes or so move on to the next step.

Step 4: Now breathe effortlessly without any interest in managing the pace or rhythm. Your attention is still on your breath, but do not be concerned with how and when to breathe in or out. . . . Just breathe comfortably, naturally. It is inevitable that your mind will wander and thoughts will enter, and that's okay. Whenever you become aware that your attention has drifted, gently turn your focus back onto your breath.

Step 5: After fifteen or twenty minutes (or even after just a few minutes, if you are pressed for time), end your breath meditation session by slowly opening your eyes and taking a moment or two to acclimate to your surroundings.

ADRENALINE AND EXERCISE

Caffeine activates the body's fight-or-flight response, triggering the release of adrenaline and cortisol just as it would for any stressful situation. Indirectly, yet equally injurious, is the role of glucose. When we eat foods high in sugar or refined carbohydrates, blood sugar spikes and then sharply decline, which then stimulates the adrenals to regulate blood sugar levels. While the cumulative effect can wreak havoc on the nervous system, the immediate impact is staggering. A Yale University study found that a single serving of a sugar-sweetened beverage caused adrenaline levels to double in adults and quadruple in children. Recent studies also show that those who suffer from obsessive/compulsive disorder (OCD), panic attacks, and anxiety may find relief with a diet low in refined sugars and simple carbohydrates. Our diet is important for another, unrelated reason. Anger-prone moments require the mental muscle of self-control or willpower, which, much like physical muscle, utilizes glucose.[6] Findings show that we are most susceptible to losing our temper when glucose levels are low or not metabolized properly.[7] A diet rich in complex carbohydrates, healthy fats, and proteins helps to reduce the fluctuation of glucose levels, and thus tilts physiology in our favor.

The stress-reducing effects of physical activity are well-documented in cross-sectional studies. Regarding anger specifically, Dr. Nathaniel Thom, a leading stress physiologist, finds that "exercise, even a single bout of it, can have a robust prophylactic effect" against the buildup of anger.[8] Prudence, however, is advised, as a worldwide study published in the American Heart Association's journal *Circulation* cautions that a person should not exercise *while* they are angry because it can triple the risk of a heart attack within the first hour.[9]

DEEP BREATHING & PROGRESSIVE MUSCLE RELAXATION

And we're back to breath. As we noted, anger is directly associated with the fight-or-flight response, and deep breathing and muscle relaxation exercises *outside* of a high-arousal situation are effective at reducing our anger *within* the situation. Notice how high-strung, nervous people carry themselves. Their bodies are often tense and stiff. The central nervous system is made up of our brain and spinal cord, and it is difficult to completely relax the mind unless we relax our physical selves as well. A daily five-minute breathing and muscle relaxation routine will be beneficial to raising your overall anger threshold. Let's take a quick look:

DEEP BREATHING

This highly effective technique can quickly relieve tension, increase oxygenation, and release toxins.

Step 1: Find a quiet spot where you can either sit comfortably or lie down. Breathe normally, focusing on your breath.

Step 2: After a minute or so, inhale deeply through your nose, filling your lungs with air.

Step 3: Once your lungs are full, slowly exhale through your mouth, with your attention on your breath. Continue to breathe in for about six seconds through your nose—hold for four to six seconds—and breathe out for about six seconds through your mouth, slowly. Repeat for several minutes.

Most of our breathing is shallow and constricted, so if you are not familiar with deep breathing, you may find it easier to practice lying down and to place your hand on your stomach; as you slowly inhale, expand your chest and abdomen and feel your hand rise and then fall with each exhale.

PROGRESSIVE MUSCLE RELAXATION

This exercise offers relief for a wide range of emotional and physiological ailments, as well as for overall stress reduction. Through practice we can better recognize when we are experiencing physical tension and learn to quickly relax those muscles to ease the accompanying stress and anxiety. We start by slowly tensing and then relaxing each muscle group and progressively working our way up the body. Here are the areas to focus on: a) each foot; b) each thigh; c) buttocks; d) stomach; e) each hand; f) each arm/bicep; g) neck and shoulders; h) jaw; and i) eyes and forehead.

- Find a quiet place to lie down and loosen any clothing that might prevent you from relaxing properly.
- Next, close your eyes and take a few deep breaths and begin to feel the tension flow out. Relax your jaw, your eyes, your forehead, and slowly scan your body, relaxing those areas that are tense and tight, and let yourself sink down. The entire first step should take no more than two minutes.
- Now, focus on your right foot. Slowly move it around and notice how that feels. Tense your foot muscles gradually until you feel as though they are as tense as possible (without causing yourself pain), count for about five seconds, and then release the tension slowly. Notice how limp your foot feels.
- Relax for 30 seconds, breathing deeply and slowly.

- Then place your attention on your left foot. Follow the same pattern of gently moving, tensing, and then releasing.
- Make sure to take 30 seconds or so to relax with some deep breaths before moving on to your calf—and in between each body part—and then progress gradually up through your body, contracting and relaxing the muscle groups along the way.

WHOLESALE VISUALIZATION

When you have the time, fold in this quick visualization exercise. Close your eyes for a moment, and get comfortable. Now imagine moving through your day anger free and the impact that has on various aspects of your life and relationships. What do you look like? How do you feel about things? What are you saying to yourself? What is your environment like? Has it changed?

Who are the people you are surrounded with? How are they looking at you? What are they saying to you? How do you react and interact with them? Now take a moment and step back into your own body, feeling both calm and energized about who you can become.

26
Getting Real with Meditation and Visualization

The previous two chapters discussed methods of visualization, breathing, and meditation. Here we incorporate these practices with two techniques to help us break free from even decades-old resentment—encased anger that encrusts us long after the situation has passed.

It's normal to think about a painful experience long after it has passed—to process it, to work through it, and perhaps to gain some insight, meaning, or message. The question researchers sought to explain is why it works sometimes—and we feel better—while other times, we become stuck and the negativity becomes more intensely ingrained. They write, "Although engaging in this meaning-making process leads people to feel better at times, it frequently breaks down, leading people to ruminate and feel worse. This raises the question: What factors determine whether people's attempts to 'work through' their negative feelings succeed or fail?"[1]

The answer to this question is concisely summarized by psychologist Guy Winch, who explains that we tend to think about painful experiences from a first-person, ego-oriented perspective—just as we experienced it, unfolding through our own eyes. However, replaying the emotionally painful memories from a third-person perspective—where we are a witness to the scene, watching ourselves, as it were, from the perspective of an outside observer, produces a profound effect. He writes, "Participants reported feeling significantly less emotional pain when they envisioned the memory using a third-person perspective than when using a first-person perspective. Further, utilizing a psychologically distant vantage point also allowed them to reconstruct their understanding of their experiences and reach new insights and feelings of closure."[2]

The findings dovetail with the essence of our discussion: The more "I" we bring into an unpleasant event, the more pain we feel. Likewise, we sink more deeply into the negativity when we remember it from our own—the first person—perspective. It is, as we know, not the situation or event that make us angry, but the degree to which we take it personally. This technique (credited to the science of neurolinguistic programming) engages the power of visualization to depersonalize the impact, producing a permanent shift in our feelings toward any situation.

THE PERCEPTUAL POSITIONS EXERCISE

1. Find a quiet place where you can relax undisturbed. Close your eyes and get comfortable.

2. Recall an experience that you feel anger about.

3. This is where you consider the situation from your own perspective, through your own eyes, as if you were looking at the other person and/or scene. How are you behaving? How are you feeling? What do you see? What do you believe about the situation? Feel the effects on your body:

the tightness, the physical tension, and the accompanying feelings—and simply observe.

4. Next, zoom out and view the situation as if you were an observer, replaying the scene once more. Talk to yourself and think about why "this person" is so angry. As we know, anger is rooted in the themes of fear and control. Ask yourself: *What exactly am I afraid of? What is the underlying fear behind the anger? What need of mine is not being met?* Spend as much time as you'd like examining your behavior and underlying motivation.

5. Now we will integrate a brief relaxation exercise to help us own our revised feelings. Feel your body and breathe (bring in the two exercises in the previous chapter on deep breathing and progressive muscle relaxation).

6. Come back into yourself and spend a few moments appreciating your choice to do something about the anger—to release it rather than to let it define you and confine you. Smile.

The following NLP (Neuro-Linguistic Programming) exercise is an enhanced spin-off of the previous technique and changes our internal representation by stripping away the intensity of the associated emotions. It accomplishes this through a dual psychological and physiological mechanism, which is explained afterward.

THE MOVIE EXERCISE

1. Find a quiet place where you can relax undisturbed. Close your eyes and get comfortable.

2. Picture yourself sitting alone, inside of a movie theater, front row and center. The screen is frozen on the first frame of the movie and it is in black and white. The first frame is a picture of you in a situation where you were previously angry. You are about to relive this moment with two (visual and auditory) differences: (1) from another vantage point and (2) with an incongruent, amusing soundtrack.

3. Imagine that you're floating out of your body and into the projection booth, so that you can see yourself (from the back) inside of the cinema and watching the screen ahead. Take a moment to take in the scene—how you're sitting, the clothes that you're wearing.

4. Now replay the memory on the screen ahead while listening to an amusing soundtrack, such as a cartoon theme or of some comedic melody. Pay attention to not only the screen, but to yourself watching the screen.

5. When you get past what is the worst of this experience, freeze the film. Float inside the movie and view everything through your own eyes, replaying it as above with the incongruent soundtrack. Afterward, run the movie at high speed, then again backward, in color, with you experiencing it in the first person. You will see everything happening in reverse; people and things will walk, talk, and move backward. The same soundtrack will play backward at top speed and the whole movie will be over quickly. Replay the scene again, and this time more quickly; and then again with the last replay taking no more than five seconds.

6. When you reach the beginning of the movie, black out the screen.

7. Repeat steps 5–8 once or twice more, until you feel little or no anger toward the person or the experience.

This technique works by disrupting our internal representation of the event, inhibiting the intensity of emotion and neutralizing the negative association. Research finds that our memories are highly malleable and possibly never completely solidify—which means that we can strengthen or weaken them at any time. When we experience a trauma, our feelings of terror and vulnerability intensify, stimulating output of adrenaline. It is the adrenaline that keeps these memories strong and intense, even days, months, or years after the event. Scientists have experimented with the drug propranolol, a beta-blocker usually used to treat heart or circulatory conditions and shown to block the production of adrenaline in nerve cells of the amygdala. Findings showed that people who received this adrenaline-blocking drug while recalling a past trauma could form a new association to the event and release themselves from the emotional pain.[3] The above-described technique is used to achieve similar results by stripping away the negative charge of any anger or fear-inducing experience.

27
In the Heat of the Moment

Anger-management techniques often fail because they are the first line of defense—we simply get worn down and worn out too easily. As the saying goes, "the best defense is a good offense," which is why our focus has been on how to avoid the need to manage our anger. With perspective, we do not have to force ourselves to remain calm when, for instance, faced with insult, because there is no pain. One does not have to fight against that which he knows to be irrelevant, much less false. Then, regardless of how low our state and how large our ego becomes in the heat of the moment, we will not succumb to anger. What does not exist cannot grow.

In the previous chapters, we explained how the brain can change, rewiring itself to establish new neural pathways, through the process called self-directed neuroplasticity.[1] Via visualization, we get the proverbial ball rolling, and as we enter the real world, the following protocol will reinforce this new wiring because to become anger free as quickly as possible, we want to limit reanimating the neurons in the *anger-response* pathway.

LET'S BE SMART

First, we want to identify when we're most at risk of going off course. When we know our triggers, we can limit the number of times we wind up facing anger-provoking scenarios. Some critical junctures—times when we're most vulnerable to falling into familiar patterns—are situation-specific, time-specific, and people-specific. If we take a detour to avoid confronting temptation, our route might be slightly longer, but we'll have a better chance of arriving safely at our destination anger free.

We should acknowledge our limitations to prevent ourselves from slipping too close to these danger zones. When we're not in the right frame of mind or don't have emotional energy to expend, it's prudent to avoid potentially confrontational conversations and situations. Moreover, it's foolish to unnecessarily drain our emotional resources. Controlling anger requires willpower, and willpower is not an infinite resource; we temporarily deplete it each time we act with restraint.[2] For example, studies found that if we resist a persuasive message, this decreases our ability to exercise self-control right afterward, and this depletion increases our vulnerability to persuasion.[3] Research concludes that people who most successfully exercise self-control usually set up their lives to minimize temptations during the day.[4]

PROTOCOL: LEVEL 1

When our ability to think clearly, or at all, is compromised, we too easily default to autopilot and fall into familiar, self-defeating, emotionally charged patterns. Setting up a protocol in advance—a prearranged course of action to follow—lets us react responsibly when we can't think and process a proper response. This is effective even when our willpower reserves are drained, because we don't have to think about what to do. In other words, our visceral reaction can be primed so that our response is thoughtful, even though it is instinctive.

The protocol in Level 1 consists of two intertwining layers, which we'll outline and then flesh out. First, we interrupt the anger-producing pattern to stop the *stimulus–response* cycle from becoming more ingrained. The interruption also moves us further away from reacting angrily, because, physiologically, it sends a biochemical signal to the nervous system to disengage the fight-or-flight response. Second, the best thing about this level is that this type of interruption relies on muscle memory—no brains necessary! In the following pages, we will discuss this concept more fully, but for now, consider muscle memory as the key behind near-flawless and near-automated performance, such as typing by an experienced typist or driving a stick shift by a seasoned driver.

Pattern Interrupt

When our emotions veer onto the anger track, we want to derail our train of thought as quickly as possible, by whatever reasonable means possible. A pattern interrupt does just this; it quickly jolts our focus to keep the locomotive from picking up steam toward an unproductive reaction. (A pattern interrupt can be any incongruent thought or gesture—snapping one's fingers, visualizing the person we're speaking to shrinking, counting backward in threes, and so on. However, we will see that one type of pattern interrupt is superior to all.) Interruptions also dampen the intensity of the original stimulus, thereby neutralizing the damage.

The Automated Muscle Memory Response

There are four levels to every type of action: (1) unconscious incompetence is when a person is unaware that he is not performing correctly; (2) conscious incompetence is when the person is aware of not having the skill set necessary to be as effective and successful as he would like to be; (3) conscious competence is when the person knows but must pay attention to what he needs to do in order to be effective; and (4) unconscious competence is when the person can perform correctly and as necessary without full, or even partial, attention. Learning to drive a stick shift effectively illustrates the four levels. At first it feels completely foreign, but the driver eventually has the skill to shift gears without consciously focusing on what he is doing; the process is now integrated into muscle memory and can be instinctually performed. Muscle memory is related to procedural memory, which is a type of unconscious, long-term memory that helps us perform specific tasks with minimal attention; and we can automatically access procedural memories without conscious awareness.

Putting it All Together

Although many traditional tools of anger management don't work, one of them remains irrefutable. The principle of *terror management* reminds us that fear impedes our ability to think. Therefore, a powerful weapon in our willpower arsenal is simply to pause and calm ourselves by breathing deeply. This is effective for two reasons: Physiologically, willpower has a biological basis, and slow, deep breathing activates the prefrontal cortex, the thinking brain. Law enforcement and military professionals combat stress with tactical breathing, which helps control the sympathetic nervous system. During a life-and-death situation, several successive deep breaths help them to think more clearly and engage more effectively.[5]

The second reason is the previously mentioned *facial feedback hypothesis*, the very act of smiling (we'll explain this in a moment) and breathing deeply sends the message to the brain that the situation is nonthreatening, and that it's not only safe to relax, but that we are already relaxed. An incongruous expression or response compels the "thinking brain" to reengage, to make sense of the conflicting emotions. Because the "external awakens the internal," our feelings will align with our behavior, instead of the opposite.

Now we'll fold in all the psychological and physiological processes into one simple protocol. Whether you are thinking about a situation, or you're in a situation that is anger or fear provoking, simultaneously smile, take a long, deep breath, and move your attention to your breath. Unclench your jaw, drop your shoulders, and just focus on your breathing. That's it. (You need only smile ever so faintly—particularly if you're in the actual situation—as you don't want others to think you're being smug or disrespectful.) When a person is anxious or angry, he may force a smile or breathe to calm himself, but doing both—smiling and breathing—gives us more than the physiological benefits of both. Together they do something almost magical: accessing memories of simultaneous smiling and (deep) breathing which are calming and pleasant, and anchoring us into this emotional state.

It is important to emphasize that our attention is on our breath, becoming mindful of how it fills our lungs and then is released gently and slowly. Typically, an anger-provoking thought or situation narrows our focus to the source of discontent. Bringing awareness to our breath instantly grounds us and interrupts the escalation of emotions. Doing this will take some practice at first, but soon enough your response will be automated, and the moment an unwelcomed thought pops up, or you find yourself in an emotionally precarious situation, your physiology will take over and free you from the grip of anger.

When all is said and done (or better, when all is not said and not done), after the initial moment has passed and we have risen above the urge to get angry, we want to take pleasure in our success. *Isn't it beautiful that I don't need to get angry anymore?* Feel the joy when you choose to remain calm (or at least in control of yourself). This isn't about taking a victory lap. Joy infuses a positive emotional charge into the action of self-control, energizing our success and animating the new and improved neural network.

PROTOCOL: LEVEL 2: *IF* YOU CAN THINK: WHAT TO SAY WHEN YOU TALK TO YOURSELF

Be real. Be honest. What you say to yourself in the heat of the moment tilts your emotional state and subsequent response. You must stay in the world of truth because any lie divides your energy and moves you into the world of falsehood, the home of the ego. You cannot, therefore, force yourself to think, *I am calm, and I don't care.* All you are doing is lying to yourself. This is one shortcoming of affirmations. Although they can certainly be powerful tools, reciting positive affirmations can be counterproductive while we're in a negative state because we charge the lie with energy. We are not whole when we suppress how we feel and deny the pain. If we feel angry, we must own that—but which part of us is angry? The ego or the soul? We feel angry, but it's not the real *us*. Rather, the false self feels angry. To maintain our authenticity while separating ourselves from the negative feeling, we instead acknowledge, *My ego is hurt. My ego is scared.* Don't ignore the pain, but rather take a moment to remind yourself that you—the soul—is not in pain, your false self is. Then ask yourself honestly and lovingly: (1) *What need of mine is not being met?* Or perhaps, *What am I afraid of?* Anger and fear are interlaced, so if you're able to identify the underlying fear, you begin to gain control over your feelings. Remember that anger often serves as a mask for emotions the ego deems too painful to acknowledge: guilt, insecurity, envy, jealousy, embarrassment, anxiety, unworthiness, emptiness . . . the list goes on. . . . Then, continue to talk to yourself. (2) *What is my objective right now?* (3) *What can I control right now?* (4) *What can I say or do to find a solution or to better the situation?* Even when self-examination yields no new insight, the process is useful because fear begins to dissipate the moment we begin to examine it.

HANG ON, HELP IS ON THE WAY!

Research shows that even in high-stress situations, we need no more than ninety seconds for our system to process any anger or fear-based emotion. This means we can clear out physiological influences and regain our full rational status in the most trying of circumstances. In *My Stroke of Insight*, Jill Bolte Taylor writes:

> Although there are certain limbic system ("emotional") programs that can be triggered automatically, it takes less than 90 seconds for one of these programs to be triggered, surge through our body, and then be completely flushed out of our bloodstream. My anger response, for example, is a programmed response that can be set off automatically. Once triggered, the chemical released by my brain surges through my body and I have a physiological experience.

Within 90 seconds from the initial trigger, the chemical component of my anger has completely dissipated from my blood and my automatic response is over. If, however, I remain angry after those 90 seconds have passed, then it is because I have chosen to let that circuit continue to run. Moment by moment, I make the choice to either hook into my neurocircuitry or move back into the present moment, allowing that reaction to melt away as fleeting physiology.[6]

No matter how visceral our initial response is, the emotion can roll right through our nervous system in just ninety seconds. We feed it only through cognitive reinforcement: selling ourselves on an impossible lie: that we can regain control by losing control.

28
The Magnitude of Gratitude

We explained how the brain establishes neural networks that reinforce emotional responses. To maximize anger control, we would do well to build up the surrounding networks that support and synergize a feeling of being calm and in control. Let's take a real-life metaphor: If a person has a damaged nerve in his leg, whereby the corresponding muscle is unable to receive a signal to contract and expand to facilitate walking, all is not lost. Certain therapies can help the patient build up the muscles around the nerve to compensate for the weakness. To create changes in the brain, we proactively engage in acts that build the shared networks, cause neurons to light up, and the dendrites, or connections, to strengthen. Of all the connections, one stands out as the one from which we get the greatest return on our investment: gratitude.

EXPECT NOTHING AND APPRECIATE EVERYTHING

The physiological and psychological benefits of gratitude are well documented. "Those who kept gratitude journals on a weekly basis exercised more regularly, reported fewer physical symptoms, felt better about their lives as a whole, and were more optimistic about the upcoming week compared to those who recorded hassles or neutral life events."[1] They were more likely to have made progress toward important personal goals (academic, interpersonal, and health-based), and reported high-energy positive moods, a greater sense of feeling connected to others, more confident about their lives, and better sleep duration and sleep quality, relative to a control group.[2] A study by psychologist Dr. Alex Wood, published in the *Journal of Research in Personality*, shows that gratitude can also reduce the frequency, duration, and intensity of depressive episodes. This is because giving and gratitude (which is itself giving—giving thanks) redirect our attention away from ourselves. When we look for ways to say thanks instead of indulging what may be our more natural impulse to complain, we break down the neural net of anger, frustration, and resentment.

The human mind can focus on only one thought at a time. If we focus on something that makes us appreciative, how likely is it that in that moment we will feel angry or unhappy? It's almost completely impossible. Gratitude is not simply a matter of looking at events through rose-colored glasses. The reticular activating system (RAS), the brain's filtering mechanism, which is located at the base of the brain, keeps us from being overwhelmed by unnecessary stimuli. Our objectives (and, in some instances, our fears) dictate what we deem important, and whether or not we unconsciously dismiss or consciously accept something. Our focus becomes our experience, our reality; and we decide what is brought into our purview. For example, when conversing at a cocktail party, you become aware of another conversation and, by shifting your attention, you can "mute" the person who is in front of you and pick up on what is being said further away. The reticular activating system hones in on what we deem important—and creates connections and possibilities that would have remained otherwise dormant.

STOP, REFLECT AND ACT

Reminding ourselves what we are grateful for, and acknowledging this *every* day, puts our focus on what we have, rather than on what we lack. We then feel, we become, we *are* more fulfilled. Take a few minutes each day to reflect on, and write down, what you are thankful for in your life. Start with your most consistent blessings—perhaps those we too often take for granted: eyes to see, fingers to touch, food to eat, and clothing to wear. Don't overthink, and don't analyze what you write. No erasing or crossing out. Just write down everything and everyone you are grateful for, as the thoughts come to mind. Now, each morning, spend a few minutes reading your gratitude list. Whenever you are so inclined—or better still, when you are less inclined—add to the list. And always remember to take a moment to appreciate what didn't happen or what didn't go wrong. Look for gratitude in every area of your life, and you'll begin to reap the benefits of a different quality of life. Recall from Chapter 8 that gratitude and joy are intimately linked. If we think about the people we know who have a sense of gratitude, we realize they're the same ones who are joyful. By contrast, those who lack appreciation usually live in a cycle of unrealized expectations and perpetual disappointment.

Moreover, consider putting an attitude of gratitude into action by not just thinking about things you are grateful for, but speaking and behaving like a grateful person. When you conduct yourself in this way, the grateful mindset more easily permeates your nature. Have in mind to take note—in real time—of five pleasant things that happen to you each day—things that you might have previously ignored or shrugged off without much thought. In the midst of each event, spend just seven seconds or so in appreciation.

Here are three other proven strategies to help transform yourself into a person of gratitude; yet equally important is to take a mental step back, by taking a few moments each morning to reflect on *who* we are, *what* we are living for, and *why*. This helps focus your thoughts, feelings, and behaviors on what is important so that distractions and potential frustrations fall naturally into proper perspective.

NOTES OF GRATITUDE

Find a quiet moment to pen a letter to someone to whom you feel especially grateful. Make sure to include as many positive details as possible about how this person has had an impact on your life. It is best to deliver this letter in person, and not on a specific occasion, such as a birthday or anniversary, but "just because." If you do, you will be privileged to witness the individual's surprise, delight, and reciprocation of affection and gratitude. This will serve to enhance your own gratitude, leading you to do this more often (even for those with whom you may have lost contact), and to continue to appreciate all the qualities you admire about this individual—and others, as well. If you're not much of a writer, don't fret. A phone call or face-to-face conversation is also effective.

WALKS OF GRATITUDE

Take a walk outdoors. It doesn't matter if there's a light drizzle or a shining sun, cold or warm outside, gear up and go. As you walk, take the time to admire the beautiful outdoors: the warm and shining sun, the dew-drenched green grass, the sounds of nature, the bright blue sky. If it's evening, cast your eyes upwards to the majesty of the night sky. Take a moment to enjoy the unparalleled perspective and humility found only in the magnificence of creation—billions of galaxies in a vast universe and ourselves.

As you continue to walk, contemplate all the blessings in your life, and your ability to appreciate all these blessings. Begin walking briskly, becoming mindful of your beating heart, swinging arms, feet hitting the ground at a steady pace, steady but rapid breathing (this integrates a powerful physiological component that reinforces our emotional state.) Now slow down, and as you make your way back home, take a moment to enjoy who you are—a person who takes time out to acknowledge what he has—a person of gratitude.

MONTAGE OF GRATITUDE

Put together a montage, collage, or assortment of pictures, photographs, and quotes of gratitude. Once a week or once a day (it should not be a chore), set aside a picture of something that brings a smile to your face or a feeling of awe and appreciation. It can be a photograph of a calming nature scene, a bright-colored butterfly, a stunning flower, your baby, your loving spouse, your elderly grandmother, your devoted mentor, a memorable vacation, a family get-together, or a recent celebration. When you have collected between fifty and one hundred photos, pictures, quotes, thoughts, and doodles, paste them all—in random order—onto a large poster. Hang this poster in a place where you will see it—and be reminded—every day of all the good in your life.

The principle of *hedonic adaptation* is the effect of growing accustomed to good in our lives. When this happens, we no longer focus on it, and as time goes by, we derive less and less satisfaction from it. When we acquire something new, we are temporarily happier, less because of its intrinsic worth, beauty or utility than because we are focused on it. The research is definitive: *Appreciation creates happiness.* We already have everything that we need to be happy, but if we don't focus on it, then we don't derive any happiness from it. To become a more grateful and thus joyful person, we need only shift our attention to what we do have rather than on what we don't.

The adage, "You don't appreciate what you have until you lose it," is more than just a quaint saying—it is a psychological truism. When you lose something of value, your focus shifts to it, and you are reminded of the joy that it brought you. It's more than ironic, though, that the pain we feel over its loss doesn't offset the pleasure it brought if we ignored it while we still had it.

If your attention is on what's missing and what's not good, then you can be surrounded by all the good fortune, blessings, and material things in the world and never find happiness. Your focus creates your thoughts, and your thoughts create your emotions. Focus on the positive and you will become a person who is filled with joy and gratitude. Focus on the negative and you will become a person who is unhappy and unpleasant. It comes down to a choice. Are you going to live your life of appreciation or expectation?

The power of focus is in play when it comes to the people in

our lives as well, courtesy of the previously noted reticular activating system. Numerous studies prove what our own experiences
have already shown us: A person intuitively senses whether we
like him, even without a single word being exchanged. When
you're speaking with a person who can bring out the worst in you,
mentally focus on his positive trait(s), and he will sense that you
like him—and, in turn, he will be inclined to like you. Benjamin
Franklin once said, "Search others for their virtues, thyself for thy
vices." Not to be outdone, President Abraham Lincoln has been
quoted as saying, "I don't like that man. I must get to know him
better." If we look for the good in another person, we will find it.

A POSITIVE GROOVE

We can make the claim that we don't control our world or even
some of our behavior. But our thoughts? Why would we choose
to focus on what disturbs us, rather than on what enthuses or in-
vigorates us? In a word: habit.

When we find ourselves in unproductive rumination, it can be
useful to interrupt it. Recall that a pattern interrupt is a specific
act that derails our train of thought to snap ourselves out of a cycle of negativity. While we are retraining our brain to focus on
all the good, it is constructive to break free from the nasty habit
many of us have of dwelling on the negative, which reinforces
competing neural networks. We can't expect to control the first
thought that enters our minds, but how much energy do we give to
it to feed on? Will we focus on it, or will we divert our attention to
something else? It's curious that we might choose to torture
ourselves, reliving painful memories and focusing on all that is
wrong, rather than to appreciate how far we've come, all that we
have, and where we would like to go.

29
The Anger Games

Disappointment exists in the space between desire and reality, whereby the more reality falls short of our desire, the more disappointed we become. The equation: *desire - reality = disappointment*. Disappointment, however, is mitigated by one factor: *expectation*. The greater the gap between *desire* and *expectation*, the more disappointment we experience. Therefore, in each situation, regardless of our desire, the more our expectations align (meaning, we expect as much) with reality, the less disappointment we experience.

Can a person be happy to learn that a loved one has broken his ribs and punctured a lung? He can—if a few minutes earlier he learned that the injured was on life support but is now expected to make a full recovery. Does he feel angry? No. To the contrary, he's filled with gratitude and joy for one reason: Reality has now exceeded his expectations (and, we'll presume, desire).

In the words of William Shakespeare, "Expectation is the root of all heartache." Expectations are a product of the ego and produce a toxic disappointment. When we manage our expectations, disappointment never fully matures into anger. Let's explain by differentiating between *desire* and *expectation*. Take, for instance, a parent whose child does poorly in school. Is the parent disappointed? Perhaps. Does the parent become angry with the child because he does poorly? It all depends on the parent's expectations of the child, and his willingness to accept his child's limitations. If the child has a learning disability *and* the parent accepts this, then anger doesn't exist. However, if the parent refuses to acknowledge his child's limitations, poor grades only serve as a constant reminder of a reality, a diagnosis that the parent refuses to face. In that case, grades become a source of constant anger and frustration. When reality unfolds in accord with expectation, even though it falls short of desire, our emotional state is not corrupted by the ego. As long as we accept the reality, we won't become angry—regardless of the experience. We recall the four stages of grief discussed in Chapter 3: denial, anger, depression, and acceptance. We cannot expect that which we refuse to accept.

MANAGING EXPECTATIONS

When reality meets or exceeds our expectations, the ego has no traction—because . . . drumroll please . . . we do not feel afraid. Anger's roots in fear are of major significance. Anger manifests when life doesn't meet our expectations, when reality surprises us, shocks us. The ego doesn't like these unpleasant surprises, because it needs to feel in control.

Let's delve more deeply into the psychological mechanics. If someone rear-ends your car, you might understandably feel shaken and angry. But if you knew that morning that it would happen later that day, when the moment came, you would feel shaken but much less surprised, and thus feel little or no anger. This is critical to understand: Anger exists because of a loss of control. Something happened that was not only undesirable, but unanticipated. By adjusting our expectations, we automatically eliminate the *element of surprise* in any given situation. Perhaps a milder example: A coworker jumps out from behind your desk—you get scared and a little angry. However, if you knew in advance where he was hiding and what his plan was, there would be no fear and hence no anger.

In these hypothetical scenarios, several important factors mitigate our anger when we have advance knowledge: (1) We reduce our shock and feeling of being out of control because we predicted it. We get to be right! Fulfilled expectations provide a layer of comfort, rather than fear or uneasiness, about even an unpleasant reality. (2) Without the element of fear, we can process the pending event more objectively and in a calm space. We can also see the ridiculous nature of an angry response, and work through our feelings in advance. (3) In the words of Albert Einstein, "In the middle of every difficulty lies opportunity." We have the luxury of time to reframe the experience in a greater context and try to find meaning in it—and perhaps look for ways to capitalize on it and turn it into an opportunity. We would not have had the presence of mind to do this in the moment.

LET'S PLAY HOW WILL I BE TRIGGERED TODAY?

We can't predict, let alone imagine, every anger-triggering scenario, but these situations and anger-provoking people do fall under some familiar themes. It's curious, if not completely ludicrous, that even though we repeatedly become angry at the same people in the same situation time and again, our ego acts as if each situation were new and unexpected—setting us up each and every time. Refusing to recognize this process is like living in la-la land. It isn't reality. Unrealized expectations are nothing more than premeditated resentment. *Why*, you may ask, *don't we naturally adjust our expectations after experiencing these "surprises," day after day, year after year, decade after decade?* A good question. Ask your ego.

If the forecaster predicts a snowstorm and you are planning on a picnic at the beach, you're not living in reality, and you're setting yourself up for utter frustration and disappointment. A wise person would plan on a different activity. Of course, forecasts being what they are, we may only get a light dusting of snow and so your ski trip might be cancelled. Fine. At least you walked out of the house with a scarf and gloves rather than sunblock and flip-flops.

We are not talking about predicting reality, but staying in reality. Here is what we can guarantee with relative accuracy: today's forecast: It will be an imperfect day. You are an imperfect person, living an imperfect life, and things in your day will be imperfect—and that's all okay. In fact, it's more than okay. It's a perfect opportunity for you to develop a greater sense of emotional resiliency, self-control, and self-respect. It is an opportunity to show the world that you are in control of yourself, and in the process, improve almost every aspect of your life and your relationships.

We might feel disrespected today—someone may cut in front of us at the supermarket or on the highway, or ignore our phone call or email. We might feel embarrassed, or someone might yell at us. Today we might feel hurt, helpless, or both. We might feel rejected, lonely, sad, or all three. Today someone might do something that makes no sense—something completely illogical and irrational. Expect it. Someone may try to take advantage of us today or insult us. We might witness an injustice. Someone may inconvenience us; a goal may be delayed; we might realize something unpleasant about ourselves or a loved one; another person's act may cause us to question the relationship or ourselves; we might become uncomfortable or feel unwanted.

Again, this is not about expecting the worst or waiting for the other shoe to drop. Rather, to quote an oft-repeated axiom: *Hope for the best, and plan for the worst.* To plan means that we are cognizant that the shoe drops many, many times every single day, in many different ways, and we can be surprised and get angry, or each time can become an opportunity to fortify our emotional health and transform our character.

30
Game Day

Becoming anger free must be your number-one priority. Don't think of this as a hobby, where you dabble only when you're inspired and it's convenient. Neural networks are competitive, so you need to activate the new response with more frequency, intensity, and duration than your anger-prone network. To help us along we want to track our progress because if you can't measure it, you can't change it. Moreover, studies show that recording and reviewing your behavior proves effective across a wide swath of areas. For example, dieters who kept a food journal lost twice as much weight over a six-month period as those who didn't; and follow-up studies conclude that they kept it off. The simple act of writing everything down a) motivates people to consume less; and b) makes it difficult for them to ignore their slip-ups.[1] Keeping a journal or charting your progress toward anger elimination is a way to move the emphasis from a single incidence of behavior to an overall pattern. It is easier, too, to sustain progress if you see evidence in writing. Memory is far more biased when you feel discouraged, and you have a harder time recalling your successes. In addition, tracking your progress allows you to adjust your tactics, because you can examine what's working and what's not working. While you may be unwavering in your pursuit, you want to be flexible in your approach.

First, we want a clear and definitive goal—and write it down. Just because you're motivated doesn't mean that you have a clear purpose. Formulating a precise definition of what you want to accomplish helps you focus on relevant activities and avoid diversions that distance you from your objectives. In fact, studies find that people are on average ten times more likely to succeed by making a firm resolution to a specific commitment.[2] Additionally, the strength of your commitment is magnified—42 percent more likely to achieve your goal—when you write it down, review your statement, and state aloud your commitment to your objective several times throughout the day. And sending weekly updates to a friend can double your rate of success.[3]

Second, success requires that for a specified period, you don't reconsider the decision to express your anger in any way. Precious energy trickles out every time you consider, *Is this a time to get angry?* There, are, of course, those who would claim that when properly expressed, anger may be appropriate. In fairness, there are a number of studies to support this position and yet, for our purposes, the debate is irrelevant, which is why, throughout this book, we have been speaking about anger in absolute terms. We recall from Chapter 5 that emotions help to energize our direction and motivate proper behavior, but only when we first see through the lens of the intellect. Let's say that 1 percent of the time anger is the proper response. In the heat of the moment, we are not able to make that call, and we will *decide* that anger is necessary closer to 99 percent of the time. Might you choose to remain calm, only to conclude after the fact that anger was, indeed, called for? Perhaps. But wouldn't you rather be right 99 percent of the time than 1 percent of the time? By taking anger off the table, we are more inclined to reframe the situation and seek solutions rather than to focus on the problem. King Solomon instructs, "Do not be eager in your heart to be angry, for anger resides in the bosom of fools."[4] Commentators explain that a fool's anger is readily available and accessible while a wise person stores his anger out of reach, so that by the time he gets to it, he has already calmed himself down. Therefore, in order to strengthen the proper neural networks, regardless of how you feel, the display of anger will be unconditionally off the table as a viable response.

Having a set time frame is also helpful because you will view whatever gains you've made appropriately—as gains—rather than considering yourself a failure because you didn't succeed in completely eradicating the behavior. Start with twenty-four hours or start with five minutes—but start, and make the goal realistic. Anger has five main measurable components: frequency, duration, intensity, trigger, and expression. You chart it any way you like, and again, don't underestimate the power of keeping a written record of your progress.

- *Frequency* How often do you get angry? Does it happen every hour? Does it happen every day? Maybe it happens several times one day, and then does not even happen for several days. Keep track of the sheer number of times you feel angry.
- *Duration* How long do you stay angry? Take note of how long it takes you to reclaim yourself and to snap out of your state.
- *Intensity* This is a little harder to measure, but you will become more aware of how intense the episodes are once you begin to

keep track of them. Using a scale from one to five can help quantify your feelings.

- *Trigger* There are always certain situations that will more easily spark our anger. This is something you should measure because you might just be surprised at the catalyst. Also, take time to identify the underlying fear at the root of the episode in order to work through it (using the process in Chapter 26).

- *Expression* What did you do with the anger? This is not a one-size-fits-all category. If you are prone to suppressing your feelings, did you choose to express yourself more openly and honestly? If you usually explode, were you able to contain yourself and calmly exit the situation?

Regarding expression, we have identified three levels of anger: (1) feeling anger in the moment; (2) acting out of anger with aggressive expression; and (3) resentment from unresolved anger. The ideal, of course, is to enjoy a wide perspective where fewer and fewer situations get caught in the ego's net. Still, if you are unable to avoid feeling angry at the time, progress can be had by restraining your anger. All too often, in the heat of the moment and out of anger, we may say or do something that further increases our feelings of embarrassment or shame. We are then forced to double down, and our anger turns into rage. We lose ourselves to our emotions because we cannot bear the pain of accepting what we're doing right now—which was in response to something else entirely. The ego goes into survival mode and re-ups the ante, again and again. The bottom line: Do whatever is necessary to avoid rage—the uncontrolled expression of anger.

Regardless of your thoughts and behavior in the moment, wiping the slate clean to rid yourself of lingering resentment, guilt, or shame is a powerful, purposeful step toward an anger free life. As we noted, taking responsibility is not about being perfect—it's what we do when we discover that we have faltered, and how we move forward to make things right after we have done wrong.

YOU'RE GOING TO LIVE ANGER FREE, GET EXCITED!

Our success coalesces around one requirement: Joy! Joy energizes our decision to live a life that is anger free. You have every reason to be excited because you're not giving anything up, and you're not losing out on anything. You are gaining in every way: maximizing your potential and actualizing your dreams, and becoming a happier, healthier person who appreciates all of the good that life has to offer you.

SPECIAL NOTE TO READERS

Although the choices we make during our lives have a strong impact on our emotional stability, severe mental illness, including anger management issues, may result from serious trauma or a genetic disposition. This mental state could affect a person's basic life functioning so significantly that his or her thoughts and behaviors fall outside the scope of genuine choice. Just as some people are physically disabled, others are emotionally impaired through no fault of their own. They neither choose nor cause their sickness, and to label them lazy or selfish is not only reprehensible, but mistaken. The tools and techniques in this book have shown to be life transforming for many people, but others will benefit from the direct guidance of a mental-health-care professional.

At what point our free will emerges remains a subject of ongoing philosophical, psychological, and biological debate, but the indisputable beginning of all change comes when we make a conscious decision to accept personal responsibility. This means that we put our ego aside and seek whatever help we need to regain control of our lives.

ACKNOWLEDGMENTS

This is my sixth book with St. Martin's Press, and I couldn't be happier to be back with the publishing house that is second to none. It is a great pleasure to acknowledge the tremendous work of the outstanding professionals with whom I have the privilege of working. First and foremost, a big thank you goes to my editor, Daniela Rapp, for her keen insights and thoughtful suggestions. Her professionalism is exceeded only by her patience. A special thanks to St. Martin's executive vice president and publisher, Jennifer Enderlin, whose continuous enthusiasm for my work and interest in this book is highly appreciated.

Sincere recognition goes to Patricia Weldygo and Tova Salb for their editorial efforts and well-honed suggestions. To Sophia Dembling, a double *thank you* for her highly thorough and superb copy editing. A special thank you to David Bendkowski for his ever-charming encouragement and to Lauren Jablonski for her always pleasant and proficient correspondence and coordination.

And to the talented people in the production, publicity, marketing, advertising, art, and sales departments, a warm and genuine acknowledgment. While your efforts for this book have just begun, you have already propelled two of my previous books onto *The New York Times* bestseller list, and helped launch a career that has gone on to impact the lives of millions of people in the United States and around the world. I am appreciative for all that you've done and continue to do.

I would like to express my gratitude to those who, throughout the years, have entrusted me to help guide them on their path to emotional wellness. I have learned much from you all, and I stand in awe of your strength, your courage, and your determination.

To my extraordinary and remarkable parents, thank you for having shaped my character; to my wonderful and loving wife, thank you for putting up with this character; and to my generally well-behaved children, who are all remarkable and amazing characters—thank you. You make it all possible and worthwhile. I am humbled and grateful to God, for His many blessings and Whose infinite kindness and benevolence have allowed this book to be written.

ENDNOTES

PART I: THE REAL REASON YOU ARE SO ANGRY

1. How Perspective Takes Shape

1. See M. Scott Peck, *The Road Less Traveled: A New Psychology of Love, Traditional Values and Spiritual Growth* (New York: Simon & Schuster, 1978), 17–19. See Roy F. Baumeister, Todd F. Heatherton, and Dianne M. Tice, *Losing Control: How and Why People Fail at Self-Regulation* (California: Academic Press, 1994). Also see Christopher Peterson and Martin E. P. Seligman, *Character Strengths and Virtues: A Handbook and Classification* (Oxford, UK: Oxford University Press, 2004).

2. In Proverbs 26:13, King Solomon wrote, "The sluggard says, 'There is a lion outside! I shall be slain in the streets!'" One might think that the coward would make such a declaration, but the wisest of men teaches us that, rather than accepting the pain and stigma of laziness, we invent fears to justify our inaction. He further explains, "The sluggard [is] wiser in his own conceit than seven men that can render a reason" (Proverbs 26:16), because his warped perception has become so ingrained that he cannot be convinced otherwise. (Laziness is not confined to physical exertion, but to the reluctance to exert effort of any type, including, most certainly, emotionally and cognitively).

2. Angry with Ourselves, Angry at the World

1. William Glasser, *Reality Therapy* (New York: Harper & Row, 1965).

2. Drew Westen, Pavel Blagov, Keith Harenski, et al., "Neural Bases of Motivated Reasoning: An fMRI Study of Emotional Constraints on Partisan Political Judgment in the 2004 U.S. Presidential Election," *Journal of Cognitive Neuroscience* 18, no. 11 (2006): 1947–1958.

3. Elliot Aronson, Timothy D. Wilson, Robert M. Akert, Samuel R. Sommers, *Social Psychology*, 9th edition (New Jersey, Pearson Education, 2015), 11.

4. Robert Fritz, *The Path of Least Resistance: Learning to Become the Creative Force in Our Own Life* (New York: Fawcett Columbine, 1989), 140.

5. Ecclesiastes 5:9.

3. Isolated from Ourselves, Disconnected from Others

1. Abraham J. Twerski, *A Formula for Proper Living: Practical Lessons from Life and Torah* (Jewish Lights Publishing, 2009).

2. See Martin L. Hoffman, "Toward a Comprehensive Empathy-Based Theory of Prosocial Moral Development" (2001), in Arthur C. Bohart and D. J. Stipek, eds., *Constructive and Destructive Behavior: Implications for Family, School, and Society.*

3. See W. Keith Campbell, Eric A. Rudich, and Constantine Sedikides, "Narcissism, Self-Esteem, and the Positivity of Self-Views: Two Portraits of Self Love," *Personality and Social Psychology Bulletin*, 358–368, http://psp.sagepub.com/content/28/3/358.short (accessed on August 30, 2016).

4. Seth Rosenthal, "The Fine Line Between Confidence and Arrogance: Investigating the Relationship of Self-esteem to Narcissism," *Dissertation Abstracts International,* 66 (5-B) (2005): 2868.

5. Wade C. Rowatt, Christie Powers, Valerie Targhetta, et al., "Development and Initial Validation of an Implicit Measure of Humility Relative to Arrogance," *Journal of Positive Psychology* 1, no. 2 (2006): 198–211.

4. Step Right Up and Choose Your Reality

1. The scenario follows interpersonal relationships, and Part IV expands the discussion to the other primary source of anger—the universe. Whether our plans are thwarted or hardships encountered, it is too easy to feel that we are being rejected by God because we are not worthy of happiness and success.

2. When the threat is not real, as in the case of a horror movie or haunted house, the fight or flight mechanism is still active to the degree that we suspend belief. However, as noted, we do not become angry because we remain in control. Therefore, in real-life scenarios, whenever our imagination gets the better of us, remind yourself that you are safe and in control, and follow the protocol in Chapter 27.

It will not happen automatically because your neural network has been habituated to responding to false alarms—becoming frightened even when we know the fear is not real. But, in a short time, you can create a different, dominant network that will override the fear-based one. The method is akin to desensitization or exposure therapy, a highly effective treatment for a range of phobic and anxiety disorders, that helps the sufferer process the situation logically and rationally, rather than emotionally.

PART II: THE COST OF LIVING, THE PRICE OF ESCAPING

5. Why Smart People Do Dumb Things

1. Antonio Damasio, *Descartes' Error: Emotion, Reason, and the Human Brain* (New York: Putnam, 1994), 193.

2. Ibid., 194.

3. Walter Mischel, Yuichi Shoda, and Philip K. Peake, "The Nature of Adolescent Competencies Predicted by Preschool Delay of Gratification," *Journal of Personality and Social Psychology* 54, no. 4 (1988): 687–696.

4. Peterson and Seligman, *Character Strengths and Virtues.* Deficiencies in self-regulation have also been linked to a broad spectrum of personal and social issues, including addiction, substance abuse, debt and bankruptcy, smoking, and obesity. See Roy H. Baumeister, Todd F. Heatherton, and Dianne M. Tice, *Losing Control: How and Why People Fail at Self-Regulation* (San Diego, CA: Academic Press, 1994).

5. G. Alan Marlatt and Judith R. Gordon eds., *Relapse Prevention: Maintenance Strategies in the Treatment of Addictive Behaviors* (New York: Guilford Press, 1985). Rajita Sinha, "Modeling Stress and Drug Craving in the Laboratory: Implications for Addiction Treatment Development," *Addiction Biology* 14, no. 1 (2009): 84–98.

6. Todd F. Heatherton and Dylan D. Wagner, *Cognitive Neuroscience of Self-Regulation Failure* (publication forthcoming), http://www.ncbi.nlm.nih.gov/pmc/articles/PMC3062191/

7. Craig A. Anderson and Brad J. Bushman, "Human Aggression," *Annual Review of Psychology* 53 (2002): 27–51.

8. Sabrina D. Bruyneel, Siegfried Dewitte, Philip Hans Franses, and Marnik G. Dekimpe, "I Felt Low and My Purse Feels Light: Depleting Mood Regulation Attempts Affect Risk Decision Making," *Journal of Behavioral Decision Making* 22, no. 2 (2009): 153–170.

9. Leah H. Somerville, Rebecca M. Jones, and B. J. Casey, "A Time of Change: Behavioral and Neural Correlates of Adolescent Sensitivity to

Appetitive and Aversive Environmental Cues," *Brain and Cognition* 72, no. 1 (2010): 124–133.

10. Viktoriya Magid, Craig R. Colder, Laura R. Stroud, et al., "Negative Affect, Stress, and Smoking in College Students: Unique Associations Independent of Alcohol and Marijuana Use," *Addictive Behavior* 34, no. 11 (2009): 973–975.

11. Rajita Sinha, "The Role of Stress on Addiction Relapse," *Current Psychiatry Reports* 9, no. 5 (2007): 388–395. Katie Witkiewitz and Nadia Aracelliz Villarroel, "Dynamic Association Between Negative Affect and Alcohol Lapses Following Alcohol Treatment," PubMed article (2009), http://www.ncbi.nlm.nih.gov/pubmed/19634957 (accessed on August 30, 2016).

12. Todd F. Heatherton, C. Peter Herman, and Janet Polivy, "Effects of Physical Threat and Ego Threat on Eating Behavior," *Journal of Personality and Social Psychology* 60, no. 1 (1991): 138–143. Michael Macht, "How Emotions Affect Eating: A Five-Way Model," *Appetite* 50, no. 1 (2008): 1–11.

13. Sherry A. McKee, Rajita Sinha, Andrea H. Weinberger, et al., "Stress Decreases the Ability to Resist Smoking and Potentiates Smoking Intensity and Reward," *Journal of Psychopharmacology* (2011). DOI: 10.1177/0269881110376694.

6. A Fight to the Death

1. "Self-Reliance," *Essays: First Series*, 1841. Ralph Waldo Emerson (1803–1882) was an American essayist, lecturer, and poet.

2. The impact of our choice carries forward. Once we commit to something, we use *adaptive self-serving biases* to support our decision. For example, after we buy a certain product, we'll be more likely to notice evidence that confirms we made the right choice.

3. Nathaniel Branden, *The Power of Self Esteem* (Florida: HCI, 1992), 14–15.

7. Reality Isn't Going Anywhere

1. David J. Levitin, "Why the Modern World is Bad for Your Brain," *The Guardian* (2015). https://www.theguardian.com/science/2015/jan/18/modern-world-bad-for-brain-daniel-j-levitin-organized-mind-information-overload

2. Adrita Arefin, "Teens and Tech: Preventing Technology Addiction," *FCD Educational Services Prevention Source e-journal* (2013) http://

myemail.constantcontact.com/E-Journal—Teens-and-Tech—Preventing
-Technology-Addiction.html?soid=1101484057590&aid=tknlYJ025Ko

3. Cited by Stephen S. Ilardi, *The Depression Cure: The 6-Step Program to
   Beat Depression without Drugs* (Cambridge, MA: Da Capo Press
   Lifelong, 2009), 6.

4. Michael Argyle, "Causes and Correlates of Happiness," *Well-Being: The
   Foundations of Hedonic Psychology*, eds. Daniel Kahneman, Ed Diener,
   and Norbert Schwartz (New York: Russell Sage Foundation, 2000),
   353–373.

5. Cited by Ilardi, *The Depression Cure: The 6-Step Program to Beat
   Depression without Drugs*, 71.

6. Annie Britton and Martin J. Shipley, "Bored to Death," *International
   Journal of Epidemiology* 39, no. 2 (2010): 323–326.

7. We are painting with a broad brush and should note that depression is a
   complicated illness that can afflict a person through no fault or failure of
   their own.

8. Stress and anxiety foster neurosis and false beliefs. "If our brain is
   distracted or under pressure, we will tend to believe statements that we
   would normally find rather dubious . . . even if we were told they were
   untrue." John A. Bargh, Mark Chen, and Lara Burrows, "Automaticity of
   Social Behavior: Direct Effects of Trait Construct and Stereotype Activa-
   tion on Action," *Journal of Personality & Social Psychology* 71, no. 2
   (1996): 230–244.

9. Abraham Maslow, *Motivation and Personality* (New York: Harper,
   1954), 46.

8. The Meaning of Pleasure, the Pleasure of Meaning

1. Bruno Silvestrini, "Trazodone: From the Mental Pain to the 'Dys-stress'
   Hypothesis of Depression," *Clinical Neuropharmacology* 12, suppl. 1
   (1989): S4–10. PMID 2568177.

2. Psalms 119:92. See also "Happy is the man whom You afflict and teach
   him Your Bible" (Psalms 94:12).

3. "You have turned my grief into dance. You have loosened my sackcloth
   and girded me with joy. So that my soul might make music to You and not
   be stilled, my God, forever will I thank you" (Psalms 30:11–12).

4. Matthias J. Koepp, Roger N. Gunn, Andrew David Lawrence, et al.,
   "Evidence for Striatal Dopamine Release during a Video Game," *Nature*
   393, no. 6682 (1998): 266–268.

5. Shawn Achor, *The Happiness Advantage: The Seven Principles of Positive Psychology That Fuel Success and Performance at Work* (New York: Crown Business, 2010), 78.

PART III: MAKING SENSE OF PAIN AND SUFFERING

9. Here Comes the Pain

1. "I can feel guilty about the past, apprehensive about the future, but only in the present can I act. The ability to be in the present moment is a major component of mental wellness" (Abraham Maslow).
2. Viktor E. Frankl, *Man's Search for Meaning.*
3. This means we have to look at our present life in the context of our multiple lives. Without exception, every recognized religion has a tradition of reincarnation. Indeed, it has even been embraced by hard science disciplines. Dr. Brian Leslie Weiss, a psychiatrist specializing in past life regression, brought many of these ideas to the forefront of modern psychology and psychiatry. In Hebrew, it is called *gilgul ha'neshamos*—literally, "the transmigration of souls through a succession of lives"—and it is mentioned in numerous places throughout the classical texts of Jewish mysticism, starting with the preeminent sourcebook of *Kabbalah*, the *Zohar*.

10. Why Good Things Happen to Bad People

1. Carl Gustav Jung, "The Symbolic Life," *Collected Works*, 18.
2. Maslow, *Motivation and Personality*, 46. Unbeknownst to many, in his later years Maslow amended his five-tier model to include a sixth tier, which places self-transcendence as a level higher than self-actualization. He writes, "The self only finds its actualization in giving itself to some higher goal outside oneself, in altruism and spirituality." Maslow, A. H., "The Further Reaches of Human Nature," *Journal of Transpersonal Psychology* (1969): 1–9.

11. Staying Sane in an Insane World

1. Genesis 12:2.
2. While God offered such assurances, at no point did Abraham ever doubt God or hesitate in carrying out His will.
3. Thomas Holmes and Richard Rahe, "Social readjustment rating scale," *Journal of Psychosomatic Research*, vol. 11 (1967): 214.

PART IV: MAKE PEACE WITH THE PAST, FOR GOOD

12. Planes of Acceptance

1. *Hamlet*, Act I, Scene iii.
2. Arnold Beisser, "Paradoxical Theory of Change," in *Gestalt Therapy Now*, eds. Joen Fagan and Irma Lee Shephard (Palo Alto: Science and Behavior Books, 1970), 77.
3. Proverbs 27:19.

14. It's Not Too Late to Have a Happy Childhood

1. As we have explained, those who lack self-esteem cannot easily give and receive love, but a qualification exists in the parent-child relationship because a parent's innate yearning to connect and give to their child helps foster a genuine love. Alas, in time, the relationship too easily sours as the parent loses control over the child and is ill-equipped to deal with feelings of hurt, rejection, or disrespect.
2. Kathleen A. Lawler, Jarred W. Younger, Rachel L. Piferi, et al., "The Unique Effects of Forgiveness on Health: An Exploration of Pathways," *Journal of Behavioral Medicine* 28. No. 2 (2005): 157.
3. Joseph LeDoux, "Emotion." In *Handbook of Physiology. 1: The Nervous System*, F. Plum, ed. (Bethesda, MD: American Physiological Society, 1987).
4. Everett L. Worthington, Charlotte Van Oyen Witvliet, Pietro Pietrini, et al., "Forgiveness, Health, and Well-being: A Review of Evidence for Emotional Versus Decisional Forgiveness, Dispositional Forgiveness, and Reduced Unforgiveness," *Journal of Behavioral Medicine* 30, no. 4 (2007): 291.
5. See Kathleen A. Lawler, Jarred W. Younger, Rachel L. Piferi, et al., "A Change of Heart: Cardiovascular Correlates of Forgiveness in Response to Interpersonal Conflict," *Journal of Behavioral Medicine* 26, no. 5 (2003): 373–393.
6. A year after Benjamin Franklin's death, his autobiography, entitled *Mémoires de la Vie Privée*, was published in Paris in March of 1791.

15. My Apologies, Please

1. See Gerhart Piers and Milton B. Singer, *Shame and Guilt: A Psychoanalytic and Cultural Study* (New York: W.W. Norton & Company, 1971).
2. Mark R. Leary, Eleanor B. Tate, Ashley Batts Allen, et al., "Self-Compassion and Reactions to Unpleasant Self-Relevant Events: The

Implications of Treating Oneself Kindly," *Journal of Personality and Social Psychology* 92, no. 5 (2007): 887–904.

3. Paul Gilbert, *The Compassionate Mind: A New Approach to the Challenges of Life* (London: Constable and Robinson, 2009).

4. Paul Gilbert, et al., "Having a Word with Yourself: Neural Correlates of Self-Criticism and Self-Reassurance," *Neuroimage* 49, no. 2 (2010): 1849–1856.

5. Eva Jonas, Jeff Schimel, Jeff Greenberg, et al., "The Scrooge Effect: Evidence that Mortality Salience Increases Prosocial Attitudes and Behavior," *Personality and Social Psychology Bulletin* 28, no. 10 (2002): 1342–1353.

PART V: HOW TO LOVE BEING ALIVE

16. A Date with Destiny

1. See Naomi Mandel and Steven J. Heine, "Terror Management and Marketing: He Who Dies with the Most Toys Wins," *Advances in Consumer Research* 26 (1999): 527–532.

17. Becoming Extraordinary

1. Karen Horney, *Our Inner Conflicts: A Constructive Theory of Neurosis* (New York: W.W. Norton & Company, 1945), 155.

2. Roy F. Baumeister and John Tierney, *Willpower: Rediscovering the Greatest Human Strength* (New York: Penguin Press, 2011), 67.

18. Escaping the Trap of Perfection

1. Functional magnetic resonance imaging (fMRI) has been used to show that the amygdala is stimulated when we make decisions couched in uncertainty. See Benedetto De Martino et al., "Frames, Biases, and Rational Decision-Making in the Human Brain," *Science* 313 (2006): 684–687.

PART VI: RECLAIMING OURSELVES AND REDEFINING OUR BOUNDARIES

21. Speak Now, or Forever Be in Pieces

1. Dana R. Carney, Amy J.C. Cuddy, and Andy J. Yap, "Review and Summary of Research on the Embodied Effects of Expansive (vs. Contractive) Nonverbal Displays," *Psychological Science* 26, no. 5 (May 2015): 657–663.

2. Pablo Brinol, Richard E. Petty, and Benjamin Wagner, "Body posture effects on self-evaluation: A self-validation approach" *European Journal of Social Psychology* 39 (2009): 1053–1064.

3. Hal R. Arkes, Lisa T. Herren, and Alice M. Isen, "The Role of Potential Loss in the Influence of Affect on Risk-Taking Behavior," *Organizational Behavior and Human Decision Processes* 42, no. 2 (1988): 181–193.

4. See Alyssa Nguyen, *Forgiveness: What's Mood Got to Do with It?* Thesis in Psychology, Humboldt State University, 2008.

5. Sybil Carrère and John Mordechai Gottman, "Predicting Divorce among Newlyweds from the First Three Minutes of a Marital Conflict Discussion," *Family Process* 38, no. 3 (1999): 293–301.

22. Successful Relationships with Impossible People

1. Douglas W. Nangle, Cynthia A. Erdley, Karen R. Zeff, et al., "Opposites Do Not Attract: Social Status and Behavioral-style Concordances and Discordances Among Children and the Peers Who Like or Dislike Them," *Journal of Abnormal Child Psychology* 32, no. 4 (2004): 425–435.

2. Daniel Goleman, *Working With Emotional Intelligence* (New York: Bantam Books, 2000).

PART VII: ADVANCED PSYCHOLOGICAL STRATEGIES TO LIVE ANGER FREE

23. The Power of Neuroplasticity

1. Brad J. Bushman, "Does Venting Anger Feed or Extinguish the Flame? Catharsis, Rumination, Distraction, Anger, and Aggressive Responding," *Personality and Social Psychology Bulletin* 28, no. 6 (2001): 724–731, as explained by Carol Tavris and Elliot Aronson, *Mistakes Were Made (But Not By Me): Why We Justify Foolish Beliefs, Bad Decisions, and Hurtful Acts* (Boston: Mariner Books, 2015), 33.

2. See Shahbaz Khan Mallick and Boyd R. McCandless, "A Study of Catharsis of Aggression," *Journal of Personality and Social Psychology* 4, no. 6 (1966): 591–596.

3. Melinda Wenner, "Smile! It Could Make You Happier," *Scientific American Mind* (September/October 2009): 14–15.

4. Maiai Szalavitz, "Sweet Solace: 10 Mostly Pleasant Truths about Pain," *Psychology Today* (September/October 2005): 74–80.

5. While the unconscious mind stores every thought, sensation, and experience, the brain is no longer able to readily access those stored memories.

6. Craig H. Bailey and M. Chen, "Morphological Basis for Long-Term Habituation and Sensitization in Aplysia," *Science* 220, no. 4592 (1983): 91–93.

7. Antonio Pascual-Leone and Fernando Torres, "Plasticity of the Senso-rimotor Cortex Representations of the Reading Finger in Braille Readers," *Brain* 116, no. 1 (1993): 39–52.

8. Proverbs 15:1.

24. Change Your Self-Concept, Change Your Life

1. Jonathan L. Freedman and Scott C. Fraser, "Compliance without Pressure: The Foot-in-the-Door Technique," *Journal of Personality and Social Psychology*, 42, no. 2 (1966): 195–202.

2. Research conducted with athletes, including Olympians and profession-als, relates that they can actually feel the muscle twinges associated with their actions as they envision themselves executing a variety of tasks. Terry Orlick and John Partington, *Psyched: Inner Views of Winning* (Canada: Coaching Association of Canada, 1986).

3. Guang Yue and Kelly J. Cole, "Strength Increases from the Motor Program: Comparison of Training with Maximal Voluntary and Imagined Muscle Contractions," *Journal of Neurophysiology* 67, no. 5 (1992): 1114–1123.

4. Roger M. Enoka, "Neural Adaptations with Chronic Physical Activity," *Journal of Biomechanics* 30, no. 5 (1997): 447–455.

5. Daniel Akst, *We Have Met the Enemy: Self-Control in an Age of Excess* (New York: Penguin Press, 2011), 14.

6. Karen Horney, *Our Inner Conflicts: A Constructive Theory of Neurosis* (New York: W.W. Norton & Company, 1995), 75–76.

7. Mark Muraven and Elisaveta Slessareva, "Mechanisms of Self-Control Failure: Motivation and Limited Resources," *Personality and Social Psychology Bulletin* 29, no. 7 (2003): 894–906.

8. Brandon J. Schmeichel and Kathleen Vohs, "Self-Affirmation and Self-Control: Affirming Core Values Counteracts Ego Depletion," *Journal of Personality and Social Psychology* 96, no. 4 (2009): 770–782.

25. Taking Advantage of the Mind/Body Connection

1. Matthew T. Gailliot, Roy F. Baumeister, C. Nathan DeWall, et al., "Self-Control Relies on Glucose as a Limited Energy Source: Willpower

Is More Than a Metaphor," *Journal of Personality and Social Psychology* 92, no. 2 (2007): 325–336.

2. Sang Hyuk Lee, Seung Chan Ahn, Yu Jin Lee, et al., "Effectiveness of a Meditation-Based Stress Management Program as an Adjunct to Pharmacotherapy in Patients with Anxiety Disorder," *Journal of Psychosomatic Research* 62, no. 2 (2007): 189–195.

3. Herbert Benson and Miriam Z. Klipper, *The Relaxation Response* (New York: HarperTorch, 2005), 78–91.

4. Herbert Benson, "The Relaxation Response: Therapeutic Effect," *Science* 278, no. 5344 (1997): 1694–1695.

5. Stuart Appelle and Lawrence E. Oswald, "Simple Reaction Time as a Function of Alertness and Prior Mental Activity," *Perceptual & Motor Skills* 38, no. 3 (1974): 1263–1268. Jagdish K. Dua and Michelle L. Swinden, "Effectiveness of Negative-Thought Reduction, Meditation and Placebo Training Treatment in Reducing Anger," *Scandinavian Journal of Psychology* 33, no. 2 (1992): 135–146.

6. Matthew T. Gailliot and Roy F. Baumeister, "The Physiology of Willpower: Linking Blood Glucose to Self-Control," *Personality and Social Psychology Review* (2007): 303.

7. Matthew T. Gailliot, et al., "Self-Control Relies on Glucose as a Limited Energy Source: Willpower Is More Than a Metaphor," *Journal of Personality and Social Psychology* 92, no. 2 (2007): 325–336.

8. Gretchen Reynolds, "Phys Ed: Can Exercise Moderate Anger?" *The New York Times,* August 11, 2010.

9. Andrew Smyth, Martin O'Donnell, Pablo Lamelas, Koon Teo, Sumathy Rangarajan, Salim Yusuf and on behalf of the INTERHEART Investigators, "Physical Activity and Anger or Emotional Upset as Triggers of Acute Myocardial Infarction," *Circulation* 134, no.15 (2016).

26. Getting Real with Meditation and Visualization

1. Özlem Ayduk and Ethan Kross, "From a Distance: Implications of Spontaneous Self-Distancing for Adaptive Self-Reflection," *Journal of Personality and Social Psychology* 98, no. 5 (2010): 809–829. http://selfcontrol.psych.lsa.umich.edu/wp-content/uploads/2017/04/SD.pdf

2. Guy Winch, "A Simple Mind Trick that Reduces Emotional Pain," *Psychology Today* September 2013.

3. John Griffiths, Gillian Fortune, Vicki Barber, et al., "The Prevalence of

Post-Traumatic Stress Disorder in Survivors of ICU Treatment: A Systematic Review," *Intensive Care Medicine* 33, no. 9 (2007): 1506–1518. DOI: 10.1007/s00134-007-0730-z.

27. In the Heat of the Moment

1. Self-directed neuroplasticity is a concept derived from the researcher Dr. Jeffrey M. Schwartz in his book *The Mind & The Brain: Neuroplasticity and the Power of Mental Force* (New York: Harper Perennial, 2003).

2. Brandon J. Schmeichel and Kathleen Vohs, "Self-Affirmation and Self-Control: Affirming Core Values Counteracts Ego Depletion," *Journal of Personality and Social Psychology* 96, no. 4 (2009): 770–782.

3. Edward Burkley, "The Role of Self-Control in Resistance to Persuasion," *Peronality and Social Psychology Bulletin* 34, no. 3 (2008): 419–431.

4. Wilhelm Hofmann, Roy F. Baumeister, Georg Förster, et al., "Everyday Temptations: An Experience Sampling Study of Desire, Conflict, and Self-Control," *Journal of Personality and Social Psychology* 102, no. 6 (2011): 1318–1335.

5. Dave Grossman and Loren W. Christensen, *On Combat: The Psychology and Physiology of Deadly Conflict in War and in Peace* (USA: PPCT Research Publications, 2004): 88.

6. Jill Bolte Taylor, *My Stroke of Insight: A Brain Scientist's Personal Journey* (New York: Viking, 2008), 146.

28. The Magnitude of Gratitude

1. Robert A. Emmons, Michael E. McCullough, and Jo-Ann Tsang, "The Measurement of Gratitude" (2003) in Shane J. Lopez and Charles R. Snyder, eds., *Handbook of Positive Psychology Assessment* (Washington, DC: American Psychological Association): 327–341.

2. Ibid.

30. Game Day

1. Jack F. Hollis, Christine M. Gullion, Victor J. Stevens, et al., "Weight Loss during the Intensive Intervention Phase of the Weight-Loss Maintenance Trial," *American Journal of Preventive Medicine* 35, no. 2 (2008): 118–126.

2. See John C. Norcross, Marci S. Mrykalo, and Matthew D. Blagys, "Auld Lang Syne: Success Predictors, Change Processes, and Self-Reported

Outcomes of New Year's Resolvers and Nonresolvers," *Journal of Clinical Psychology* 58, no. 4 (2002): 397–405. PubMed PMID: 11920693.

3. Dr. Gail Matthews, Professor of Psychology, Dominican University in California. Findings presented in May 2015 at the Ninth Annual International Conference of the Psychology Research Unit of Athens Institute for Education and Research (ATINER).

4. Ecclesiastes 7:9.

ABOUT THE AUTHOR

David J. Lieberman, Ph.D., is an award-winning author and internationally recognized leader in the fields of human behavior and interpersonal relationships. His twelve books, which have been translated into twenty-six languages and include two *New York Times* bestsellers, have sold more than three million copies worldwide. Dr. Lieberman's works have been featured in hundreds of major publications, and he frequently appears as a guest expert on national media outlets, including multiple appearances on such shows as *The Today Show*, *The View*, and *Fox & Friends*.

Dr. Lieberman is known for his penetrating insights into human behavior, and his ability to offer practical psychological tools to help people lead happier, healthier, and more productive lives. He has trained personnel in every branch of the United States military, the FBI, and the NSA, and his instructional video is mandatory viewing for psychological operations (PSYOPS) graduates. He also teaches the psychological protocol of self-mastery to government negotiators, mental-health professionals, and Fortune 100 executives around the world; organizations and corporations in more than thirty-five countries use his techniques.

Contact Dr. Lieberman at: DrLieberman@Live.com Website: DrDavidLieberman.com